the beginner's KETO meal plan

the beginner's
KETO
meal plan

A Six-Week Guide to Starting Your Keto Diet the Right Way

KASSEY CAMERON

creator of Keto4Karboholics

PAGE STREET
PUBLISHING CO.

PAGE STREET
PUBLISHING CO.

First published in 2020 by
Page Street Publishing Co.
27 Congress Street, Suite 105
Salem, MA 01970
www.pagestreetpublishing.com

Distributed by Macmillan, sales in Canada by The Canadian Manda Group.

25   24   23   22   21   3   4   5   6

ISBN-13: 978-1-64567-094-0
ISBN-10: 1-64567-094-5

Library of Congress Control Number: 2019957249

Cover and book design by Rosie Stewart for Page Street Publishing Co.
Photography by Donna Crous

Printed and bound in the United States

Dedication

To my husband, Eric, who not only encourages me and pushes me to continue to grow, but also selflessly volunteers to be my taste tester. Without him, none of this would have been possible.

To Aryia and Cooper, my children, thank you for all your patience in sharing your mom's time so that I could make this dream a reality.

And finally, to my followers that have supported me and cheered me on from the beginning.

CONTENTS

My Story

Hi, my name is Kassey! Having successfully lost 60 pounds (27 kg)—and having kept it off for over three years—I wanted to help others do the same by sharing my successes and struggles so that they don't have to find their way blindly. Over the last three years I have worked with over 70,000 people to help them adopt a Ketogenic lifestyle, not only to lose weight, but to lead healthier lives.

I am not a prepackaged, frozen dinner or bland chicken and brown rice girl. I want flavor, I want fresh ingredients, I want cultural dishes—I want it all. So one July day I decided to make my own recipes. Over time I learned that it wasn't "I can't have ___," but rather "I choose not to have ___." What is most surprising to me is that by sharing my story and recipes online, I developed a following of men and women that shared my same vision, and from this my Keto4Karboholics website was born.

In a world obsessed with carbs, it's difficult to get started. That feeling of helplessness—of not knowing what to turn to when you need a quick snack, an appetizer for a party or a cake for a birthday, after eating a very different way most of your life—is real. Habits and traditions are so strongly centered on food that it can seem almost impossible to break away. I won't sugarcoat it—and not just because I gave up sugar—but the first week is hard. During my first week of Keto, I told my husband that I would rather be fat and happy with my French fries than live a life carbless. But that wasn't true, was it? I was overweight—that part was true. But I wasn't happy.

Having a science background, I knew how it worked. I understood the physiological responses food has on the body. And I told myself, "Kassey, you NEED a change. And this is it. You can't give up in a week when you gave yourself YEARS to try to make the way you were eating before work. While the weight loss may not always be fast, a loss is a loss and your health is worth more than short-term cravings. You can do anything for seven days." I am a strong woman that has birthed two children, and I was NOT going to let food control my life anymore. And so I made the commitment to get through those first seven days. And at the end I was feeling like I had more energy, my bloat was gone and the number on the scale was going down. I was empowered to keep going. And the rest is history.

This book is meant to share with you all the pieces of the puzzle that added up to my success, and the success of tens of thousands of men and women. This includes:

- Having a meal plan structured around a well-balanced Ketogenic diet that takes the guesswork out of meal planning.
- Macros. Learning what they are and how they are used to ensure you are getting in the proper number of calories, micronutrients and macronutrients (carbs, fats and protein).
- Learning portion control. Weighing a total recipe and dividing that weight by the amount of servings the recipe lists helps you to understand what you need in order to fuel your body properly.
- Never feeling deprived. This is not a starvation diet. This is not a quick fix. This is a sustainable way of eating that offers variety.

Let's get started!

What Is Keto?

The Ketogenic diet revolves around the body entering into a metabolic state known as ketosis. Getting your body into this state requires knowledge of what your body actually needs in terms of calories, carbohydrates, fats and protein. This largely works by drastically reducing carbohydrate intake and moderately limiting protein intake. In this state, your body does a few things differently, mainly utilizing the fat in your body and the fats that you consume as energy. This new source of calories burns cleaner and longer in the body than glucose and helps most individuals to experience more consistent energy levels throughout the day, decreased inflammation in the body, and also helps to shed excess body weight.

The Basics

Fats

The Ketogenic diet is a high-fat diet, but not in the way most people think. It is not an all-you-can-eat fat buffet where you are eating hundreds of grams of fat a day. Instead, a large percentage of your calories are coming from good sources of fat that complement your calories from protein and carbs. The Ketogenic diet, when done properly, is full of fresh vegetables, good fats, dairy and meats. There are many great vegetables that provide vital vitamins, fiber, magnesium, etc. that are low-carb/Keto-friendly. In addition to veggies, you can also have some berries in moderation. Many fruits are just too high in carbs, so they are not good options for those following a Keto lifestyle.

Proteins

While you do want to be taking in a high percentage of fats on the Ketogenic diet, you do NOT want to be eating too much protein. This is a common misconception with the diet. You cannot have whatever you want when it comes to protein—you need to be eating calorically appropriate to your body's needs and activity level. Even though meat is generally zero carbs, it has calories and protein. Consuming too much protein will put you at a disadvantage as it can negatively impact your state of ketosis, which can create weight loss stalls.

Macronutrients (Macros)

Tracking your macros—the breakdown of your calories—is important for long-term success. There are a number of macro calculators available online that can help you determine how many calories, fat, carbohydrates and protein are required to fuel your body based on your height, weight, age, gender and activity level and your nutrition goals: weight loss, weight maintenance or bulking. For many people using the Keto diet to aid in weight loss, changing to this way of eating will require a reduction in total calories—the majority of which will come from the elimination of carbohydrates. Some may need to limit their protein intake, but this is different for each person depending on their activity levels.

In addition to your moderately low protein intake, you want to make sure you are getting the most out of your macronutrients and you are consuming a good number of micronutrients. What are micronutrients? Micronutrients are the vitamins and minerals you need to maintain a healthy, balanced diet. This means that bacon and bulletproof coffee alone are not going to cut it. Leafy green vegetables, avocados, broccoli and cauliflower are Ketogenic staples and provide you with essential fiber, vitamins and minerals to help you achieve optimal health. People who do not consume proper micronutrients often complain of constipation, fatigue, muscle cramps, headaches and hair loss, among other issues. These complaints are not only common for those not getting in their micronutrients on the Ketogenic diet, but all diets. Vegetables are a very good source of magnesium, potassium and fiber and cannot and should not be replaced by supplements alone. No supplement can provide you with a better source of vitamins and minerals than just eating a diet full of vegetables.

In conclusion, the Ketogenic diet is a high-fat, moderately low-protein and low-carbohydrate diet. When followed appropriately, it includes healthy sources of fats from avocados, coconut oil, MCT oil and dairy; micronutrients from vegetables such as spinach, cauliflower and broccoli; and protein from meats, fish, eggs and nuts. It is a sustainable lifestyle that, while restrictive in carbohydrates, allows for a great many other options to leave you feeling satisfied and living a healthier life.

How the Program Works

1. Calculate your macros and eat within them.

You want to get as close to your required fats as you can every day. This is incredibly important. You never want to go over your allotted protein. You can come in under protein by 10 grams, but not over. Carbs are not a goal, but a limit. You can come in under carbs. You need to make sure you do not go over in calories. You want to try to get close to your goal each day—undereating will not do you any favors.

2. Track your food in advance.

This is probably one of the biggest tips I can give you. It is so difficult to track your food after you eat—especially when you are new to the diet—because you might underestimate calories or other macros and realize you ate a day's worth of macros just with breakfast. You can't un-eat something, so tracking what you will eat the night before helps you to adjust your day to meet your needs.

I am someone who has always needed a dessert each day to not feel restricted. So I track my dessert first. Then I add in my dinner and breakfast. Normally I use whatever is remaining to make a cauliflower rice bowl or a spinach salad for lunch, since both start as very low-calorie and are low in macros. I can then add to it to get in the remaining macros I need. If you need more fats, add avocado, cheese, dressing or oil. If you need more protein, add meats, nuts or eggs. As you become more comfortable tracking, you can start branching out to different lunches.

3. Stay hydrated and replenish your electrolytes.

The Ketogenic diet is a natural diuretic. For those unfamiliar with this term, that means that the body naturally wants to rid itself of the excess fluids it is holding on to. For the Keto diet, the most important electrolytes we will focus on are sodium, magnesium and potassium. You will want to make sure you are hydrated and replenishing electrolytes throughout the day. This will change from person to person, so it takes some trial and error to find your sweet spot. While this is not meant to be taken as medical advice, these are commonly recommended amounts of each. You can always discuss your specific needs with your health care provider.

Potassium: You need about 4,000 milligrams a day. If you follow my Meal Plan (included on pages 15 to 21) to a T, you will get a good amount of it, but you may still need a bit more. Start by supplementing with an additional 99 milligrams a day and up it to 300 milligrams a day if needed.

Magnesium: You need about 400 milligrams a day. Just like with potassium, you do get a good amount from my Meal Plan. When supplementing, it's generally okay to start with 200 to 250 milligrams twice a day.

Sodium: You need about 2,000 milligrams a day. You will consume a good amount of that from the Meal Plan. If you need to increase your sodium intake, try drinking more broth or having a "lick" of pink salt.

4. Don't focus solely on the scale!

The scale is not the only measurement of success. Our bodies are changing in more ways than just the scale, and body measurements are important. I recommend taking a piece of yarn and measuring your waist. Cut the yarn and tape it on a door. Repeat this every week and watch as it gets smaller! You should also focus on other victories—more energy, a clearer complexion, etc.

5. Do NOT give up.

We know what giving up gets us. Now it's time to believe in yourself. You DESERVE to give this your all. This isn't a punishment. Consistently taking care of your body will bring results—don't cheat yourself by giving up before you have a chance to succeed.

Foods and Products to Avoid

Processed Meats

Most processed meats contain sugar. Over time this will stall your weight loss. Bacon is the only processed meat you should have while following my program, and it should be consumed in moderation. Avoid pepperoni, salami and lunch meats.

Atkins® and Quest Nutrition® Products

These may be low carb, but they are not Keto friendly. They will cause stalls and potentially weight gain because many of their ingredients contribute to blood glucose spikes. These spikes can kick your body out of ketosis.

Premade Low-Carb or Keto Breads

These breads have ingredients that cause stalls due to blood glucose spikes 99 percent of the time.

Sugar

This may seem obvious, but read all ingredient labels and stay clear of products that list sugar as an ingredient, in all its forms:

- Agave Nectar
- Barbados Sugar
- Barley Malt
- Barley Malt Syrup
- Beet Sugar
- Brown Sugar
- Buttered Syrup
- Cane Juice
- Cane Juice Crystals
- Cane Sugar
- Caramel
- Carob Syrup
- Caster Sugar
- Coconut Palm Sugar
- Coconut Sugar
- Confectioners' Sugar
- Corn Sweetener
- Corn Syrup
- Corn Syrup Solids
- Date Sugar
- Dehydrated Cane Juice

- Demerara Sugar
- Dextrin
- Dextrose
- Evaporated Cane Juice
- Free-Flowing Brown Sugars
- Fructose
- Fruit Juice
- Fruit Juice Concentrate
- Glucose
- Glucose Solids
- Golden Sugar
- Golden Syrup
- Grape Sugar
- High-Fructose Corn Syrup
- Honey
- Icing Sugar
- Invert Sugar
- Malt Syrup
- Maltodextrin
- Maltol

- Maltose
- Mannose
- Maple Syrup
- Molasses
- Muscovado
- Palm Sugar
- Panocha
- Powdered Sugar
- Raw Sugar
- Refiner's Syrup
- Rice Syrup
- Saccharose
- Sorghum Syrup
- Sucralose
- Sucrose
- Sugar
- Sweet Sorghum
- Syrup
- Treacle
- Turbinado Sugar
- Yellow Sugar

Artificial Sweeteners

You want to avoid aspartame, maltitol and Keto sugars called blends. While a small amount of maltitol would not cause a stall in most people, it can cause problems if it is not consumed in moderation. Keto sugar blends are mixtures of Keto-friendly sweeteners and sugar, like when something like erythritol is blended with sugar. Avoid these.

Water Enhancers

Crystal Light, MiO (unless it is one that only contains stevia) and drops similar to these use poor sugar substitutes that can spike your blood glucose and can kick you out of ketosis. These need to be avoided.

Meal Plan by Week

The meal plan can be followed as is for a family of four or adjusted for those cooking for more or fewer people. If you want to repeat a day until the food is gone, you can do that as well—it cuts down on cooking! This meal plan is meant to be a great base to build on in order to hit your individual macros. Add a sauteed veggie or salad to your dinner each night to ensure you are getting in plenty of micronutrients.

If you happen to not like a specific meal that's recommended on a certain day, you can always swap it out with another recipe as long as it fits within your macros. I included a few bonus recipes that aren't included in the meal plan to give you even more options for making swaps.

WEEK 1

Monday

Breakfast	Maple Nut Faux-tmeal (page 32)
Lunch	BBQ Cauliflower Rice Bowl (page 78)
Dinner	Mouthwatering Italian Chicken (page 88)
Snack	Double Chocolate Chip Cookies (page 190)

Tuesday

Breakfast	Double Chocolate Muffins (page 33)
Lunch	Jalapeño Popper Soup (page 59)
Dinner	Beef Bourguignon (page 122)
Snack	Double Chocolate Chip Cookies (page 190)

Wednesday

Breakfast	Double Chocolate Muffins (page 33)
Lunch	Jalapeño Popper Soup (page 59)
Dinner	Tuscan Salmon (page 156)
Snack	Strawberry Shortcake for Two (page 189)

Thursday

Breakfast	Maple Nut Faux-tmeal (page 32)
Lunch	BBQ Cauliflower Rice Bowl (page 78)
Dinner	Grilled Margherita Chicken (page 100)
Snack	Double Chocolate Chip Cookies (page 190)

Friday

Breakfast	Maple Nut Faux-tmeal (page 32)
Lunch	BBQ Cauliflower Rice Bowl (page 78)
Dinner	Bacon Chicken Caesar Casserole (page 84)
Snack	Double Chocolate Chip Cookies (page 190)

Saturday

Breakfast	Double Chocolate Muffins (page 33)
Lunch	Jalapeño Popper Soup (page 59)
Dinner	Cajun Pork Chops (page 133)
Snack	Double Chocolate Chip Cookies (page 190)

Sunday

Breakfast	Double Chocolate Muffins (page 33)
Lunch	Jalapeño Popper Soup (page 59)
Dinner	Roasted Greek Salmon (page 168)
Snack	Strawberry Shortcake for Two (Page 189)

WEEK 2

Monday

Breakfast	Lemon Poppy Delight Muffins (page 37)
Lunch	Broccoli Salad 2.0 (page 60)
Dinner	Fiesta Casserole (page 92)
Snack	That Dough Though Cookie Dough Fat Bombs (page 181)

Tuesday

Breakfast	Creamy Peanut Butter Banana Chocolate Frappe (page 42)
Lunch	Paella Bowls (page 66)
Dinner	Crispy Chicken Tenders with Creamy Spinach (page 95)
Snack	Snickers Chia Seed Pudding (page 197)

Wednesday

Breakfast	Lemon Poppy Delight Muffins (page 37), Chocolate Lover's Bulletproof Hot Cocoa (page 47)
Lunch	Paella Bowls (page 66)
Dinner	American Goulash (page 146)
Snack	That Dough Though Cookie Dough Fat Bombs (page 181)

Thursday

Breakfast	Creamy Peanut Butter Banana Chocolate Frappe (page 42)
Lunch	Broccoli Salad 2.0 (page 60)
Dinner	Caribbean Shrimp (page 163)
Snack	Snickers Chia Seed Pudding (page 197)

Friday

Breakfast	Lemon Poppy Delight Muffins (page 37) , Chocolate Lover's Bulletproof Hot Cocoa (page 47)
Lunch	Paella Bowls (page 66)
Dinner	Creamy Tortilla Soup (page 134)
Snack	That Dough Though Cookie Dough Fat Bombs (page 181)

Saturday

Breakfast	Creamy Peanut Butter Banana Chocolate Frappe (page 42)
Lunch	Broccoli Salad 2.0 (page 60)
Dinner	Sticky Bourbon Chicken (page 91)
Snack	Snickers Chia Seed Pudding (page 197)

Sunday

Breakfast	Lemon Poppy Delight Muffins (page 37) , Chocolate Lover's Bulletproof Hot Cocoa (page 47)
Lunch	Paella Bowls (page 66)
Dinner	Shrimp Fantastico (page 175)
Snack	That Dough Though Cookie Dough Fat Bombs (page 181)

WEEK 3

Monday

Breakfast	Caramel-Pecan Cinnamon Rolls (page 27)
Lunch	Bacon and Spinach Calzone (page 77)
Dinner	Loaded Halloumi Fries (page 130)
Snack	Candy Bar Fat Bombs (page 185)

Tuesday

Breakfast	Mini Mexican Crustless Quiches (page 24)
Lunch	Chinese-Style Fried Rice (page 64)
Dinner	Loaded Chunky Chili (page 118), "Hold the Corn" Corn Bread (page 121)
Snack	Candy Bar Fat Bombs (page 185)

Wednesday

Breakfast	Caramel-Pecan Cinnamon Rolls (page 27)
Lunch	Summer Antipasto Salad (page 63)
Dinner	Roasted Greek Salmon (page 168)
Snack	Candy Bar Fat Bombs (page 185)

Thursday

Breakfast	Mini Mexican Crustless Quiches (page 24)
Lunch	Chinese-Style Fried Rice (page 64)
Dinner	Taco Pie (page 152)
Snack	Candy Bar Fat Bombs (page 185)

Friday

Breakfast	Mini Mexican Crustless Quiches (page 24)
Lunch	Summer Antipasto Salad (page 63)
Dinner	Chicken Divan Casserole (page 104)
Snack	Candy Bar Fat Bombs (page 185)

Saturday

Breakfast	Mini Mexican Crustless Quiches (page 24) , Chocolate Lover's Bulletproof Hot Cocoa (page 47)
Lunch	Chinese-Style Fried Rice (page 64)
Dinner	Stuffed Pepper Soup (page 126)
Snack	Candy Bar Fat Bombs (page 185)

Sunday

Breakfast	Chocolate Lover's Bulletproof Hot Cocoa (page 47)
Lunch	Chinese-Style Fried Rice (page 64)
Dinner	Sweet and Spicy Salmon (page 167)
Snack	Cannoli Fat Bombs (page 196)

WEEK 4

Monday

Breakfast	Chocolate Lover's Bulletproof Hot Cocoa (page 47)
Lunch	The Best Mac and Cheese (page 54)
Dinner	Baked Stuffed Steak (page 150)
Snack	Bakery-Style Chocolate Chip Cookies (page 182)

Tuesday

Breakfast	Breakfast Faux-Granola Bars (page 34)
Lunch	Strawberry Bliss Salad (page 70)
Dinner	Keto Shepherd's Pie (page 141)
Snack	Bakery-Style Chocolate Chip Cookies (page 182)

Wednesday

Breakfast	Breakfast Faux-Granola Bars (page 34)
Lunch	The Best Mac and Cheese (page 54)
Dinner	Pecan-Crusted Maple Salmon (page 159)
Snack	Bakery-Style Chocolate Chip Cookies (page 182)

Thursday

Breakfast	Breakfast Faux-Granola Bars (page 34)
Lunch	Strawberry Bliss Salad (page 70)
Dinner	Pizza Pot Pie (page 137)
Snack	Cream Cheese Brownie for One (page 194)

Friday

Breakfast	Breakfast Faux-Granola Bars (page 34)
Lunch	The Best Mac and Cheese (page 54)
Dinner	Creamy Garlic Chicken (page 108)
Snack	Bakery-Style Chocolate Chip Cookies (page 182)

Saturday

Breakfast	Breakfast Faux-Granola Bars (page 34)
Lunch	Strawberry Bliss Salad (page 70)
Dinner	Lick-Your-Plate Good Burger (page 145)
Snack	Bakery-Style Chocolate Chip Cookies (page 182)

Sunday

Breakfast	Chocolate Lover's Bulletproof Hot Cocoa (page 47)
Lunch	Strawberry Bliss Salad (page 70)
Dinner	Creamy Italian Shrimp (page 160)
Snack	Bakery-Style Chocolate Chip Cookies (page 182)

WEEK 5

Monday

Breakfast	Burrito Breakfast Bowl (page 38)
Lunch	BLT Bowl (page 56)
Dinner	Mozzarella Meatball Casserole (page 112)
Snack	Chocolate Peanut Butter Fat Bombs (page 184)

Tuesday

Breakfast	Pumpkin Maple-Glazed Donuts (page 45)
Lunch	Creamy Tomato Soup (page 55)
Dinner	Cranberry Baked Brie Chicken (page 103)
Snack	Chocolate Peanut Butter Fat Bombs (page 184)

Wednesday

Breakfast	Burrito Breakfast Bowl (page 38)
Lunch	Creamy Tomato Soup (page 55)
Dinner	Greek Meatballs (page 149)
Snack	Whoopie Pies (page 178)

Thursday

Breakfast	Burrito Breakfast Bowl (page 38)
Lunch	Creamy Tomato Soup (page 55)
Dinner	Slow Cooker Curry Chicken (page 99)
Snack	Whoopie Pies (page 178)

Friday

Breakfast	Burrito Breakfast Bowl (page 38)
Lunch	Cobb Salad 2.0 (page 74)
Dinner	Dynamite Shrimp (page 171)
Snack	Seriously-Even-Better Magic Bars (page 199)

Saturday

Breakfast	Chocolate Lover's Bulletproof Hot Cocoa (page 47)
Lunch	Cobb Salad 2.0 (page 74)
Dinner	Speedy Meatloaf (page 125)
Snack	Chocolate Peanut Butter Fat Bombs (page 184)

Sunday

Breakfast	Pumpkin Maple-Glazed Donuts (page 45)
Lunch	Creamy Tomato Soup (page 55)
Dinner	Pan-Seared Tomato Basil Haddock (page 172)
Snack	Whoopie Pies (page 178)

WEEK 6

Monday

Breakfast	Mean Green Smoothie (page 46)
Lunch	Veggie Minestrone Soup (page 73)
Dinner	Kassey's Keto Kasserole (page 85)
Snack	OMG Bars (page 186)

Tuesday

Breakfast	Coffee Cake Swirl Muffins (page 48)
Lunch	Veggie Minestrone Soup (page 73)
Dinner	Bacon Chicken Caesar Casserole (page 84)
Snack	OMG Bars (page 186)

Wednesday

Breakfast	Everything Bagels (page 51)
Lunch	Veggie Minestrone Soup (page 73)
Dinner	Lemon Garlic Butter Scallops (page 164)
Snack	Chocolate Peanut Butter Fat Bombs (page 184)

Thursday

Breakfast	Coffee Cake Swirl Muffins (page 48)
Lunch	Veggie Minestrone Soup (page 73)
Dinner	Sweet and Sour Chicken (page 87)
Snack	Chocolate Peanut Butter Fat Bombs (page 184)

Friday

Breakfast	Coffee Cake Swirl Muffins (page 48)
Lunch	Veggie Minestrone Soup (page 73)
Dinner	Chicken Pot Pie (page 96)
Snack	Chocolate Peanut Butter Fat Bombs (page 184)

Saturday

Breakfast	Everything Bagels (page 51)
Lunch	Zuppa Toscana (page 81)
Dinner	Maple-Bourbon Meatballs (page 115)
Snack	OMG Bars (page 186)

Sunday

Breakfast	Maple Bacon Donuts (page 31)
Lunch	Spanakopita (page 69)
Dinner	Deconstructed Garlic Steak Kabobs (page 153)
Snack	OMG Bars (page 186)

BREAKFAST OF CHAMPIONS

While I am not one to turn my nose up at some bacon and a bulletproof coffee, sometimes a gal needs to brunch! And that means pastries, porridges and other Keto breakfast staples that you thought were lost to you forever. From savory quiches to fluffy, decadent Dutch pancakes, there is a breakfast option in this chapter to please any desire, without guilt.

MINI MEXICAN CRUSTLESS QUICHES

MAKES: 10 quiches

1 QUICHE: 255 Calories, 22 g Fat, 2 g Carbs, 13 g Protein

|||||||||||||||||||||||||||||||||||||||||||

2½ tsp (8 g) garlic powder

1¼ tsp (3 g) onion powder

2½ tsp (5 g) oregano

5 tsp (10 g) black pepper

5 tsp (12 g) erythritol

5 tbsp (35 g) chili powder

2½ tsp (7 g) paprika

1¼ tsp (3 g) red pepper flakes

5 tsp (30 g) salt

7½ tsp (13 g) cumin

½ lb (230 g) ground beef

5 large eggs

1 cup (240 ml) heavy cream

¼ cup (60 ml) mayo

¼ cup (37 g) red bell pepper, diced

¼ cup (37 g) green bell pepper, diced

3 tbsp (45 g) green onions

3 cups (90 g) spinach, chopped

1½ cups (170 g) Cheddar cheese, shredded, divided

When you think eggs for breakfast, you might think of the obvious: scrambled, fried or, if you are feeling fancy, poached. But these Mini Mexican Crustless Quiches are anything but obvious! A delicious escape from your boring morning eggs and filled with peppers, onions, spinach and an amazing blend of Mexican spices, these fluffy and flavor-filled quiches will have you saying olé to your day!

Preheat the oven to 350°F (176°C). Grease a muffin tin.

To make the taco seasoning, in a small bowl combine the garlic powder, onion powder, oregano, black pepper, erythritol, chili powder, paprika, red pepper flakes, salt and cumin. Set aside 1 teaspoon of the seasoning and save the remaining for another use.

In a medium skillet, add the ground beef and 1 teaspoon of the taco seasoning, cooking until the meat has browned. Set aside. Do not drain the cooking fat.

In a medium bowl, whisk the eggs, cream and mayo. Fold in the bell peppers, onions, spinach, beef and 1 cup (113 g) of the cheese. Pour the mixture evenly into the greased muffin tins. Top with the remaining cheese.

Bake for 12 to 15 minutes, or until the center is set when gently shaken.

CARAMEL-PECAN CINNAMON ROLLS

MAKES: 8 cinnamon rolls

1 ROLL: 267 Calories, 24 g Fat,
3 g Carbs, 8 g Protein

||||||||||||||||||||||||||||||||||||||||||||||||||

ROLLS

1½ cups (170 g) shredded part-skim mozzarella cheese

2 oz (60 g) cream cheese

1 large egg

2 tbsp (15 g) brown sugar replacement (I recommend Swerve) or erythritol

1¼ cups (130 g) almond flour

2 tbsp (15 g) ground flaxseed

1 tbsp (15 ml) vanilla extract

½ tsp baking soda

Pinch of salt

CARAMEL SAUCE

¼ cup (60 g) butter

6 tbsp (42 g) erythritol

2 tbsp (15 g) brown sugar replacement (I recommend Swerve) or erythritol

½ cup (120 ml) heavy cream

¼ tsp xanthan gum

1 tbsp (15 ml) vanilla extract

¼ tsp salt

2 tbsp (30 ml) water

Let's face it, a good, gooey, warm cinnamon roll is one of the best ways to start your morning. Now you can enjoy that Cinnabon copycat with all the deliciousness and a tenth of the carbs! These are so good that even your non-Keto friends—don't worry, by the end of this cookbook you will have converted them all—will be asking for seconds!

To make the rolls, melt the mozzarella and cream cheese together in a microwave-safe bowl for 1 minute. Stir, then microwave for an additional 30 seconds. Repeat this step if necessary until the mixture is smooth. Add the egg and mix until well blended. Add the sugar replacement, flour, flaxseed, vanilla, baking soda and salt. Using your hands, mix until thoroughly combined. This should take about 3 to 4 minutes.

Place a piece of greased parchment paper on a flat surface and scrape the dough onto the center. Place another piece of greased parchment paper on top of the dough and roll it into a large rectangle.

To make the caramel sauce, in a medium saucepan set over medium heat, combine the butter, erythritol and sugar replacement. Bring to a boil and cook for 3 to 5 minutes. Be careful not to burn. Remove from the heat and add the cream. The mixture will bubble vigorously. Sprinkle with the xanthan gum and whisk to combine. Add the vanilla and salt. Return the mixture to heat and boil for 1 minute. Let cool to lukewarm and stir in the water until well combined.

Remove the parchment paper on the top of the dough, and add the filling by sprinkling the cinnamon and sugar replacement evenly over the dough, topping it with the chopped pecans and drizzling it with the caramel sauce.

Carefully take the bottom piece of the parchment paper and use it to roll the dough into a log—do not touch the dough with your hands, as it is very sticky. After each turn, press down the dough. Place the rolled dough in the freezer while the oven preheats.

(continued)

FILLING

1 tbsp (7 g) cinnamon

4 tbsp (30 g) brown sugar replacement (I recommend Swerve) or erythritol

½ cup (55 g) pecans, chopped

1 tbsp (15 ml) Caramel Sauce

FROSTING

2 oz (60 g) cream cheese

3 tbsp (45 g) butter, melted and cooled

¼ to ½ cup (30 to 60 g) powdered erythritol

1 tsp vanilla extract

Preheat the oven to 400°F (204°C). Grease a metal pie plate.

Using a sharp knife, slice the log into 8 equal-sized portions to create the rolls. Place the rolls on the pie plate, cut side down, and bake for 20 to 25 minutes, or until the dough browns. The rolls will still be a little soft, but they will harden as they cool.

To make the frosting, use a small blender or hand mixer to blend the cream cheese, butter, powdered erythritol and vanilla. Allow the rolls to cool, then frost.

TIP: To make the caramel sauce extra creamy, cool the caramel for 5 minutes, then blend with an immersion blender or standard blender on high for 30 seconds. Any extra caramel sauce will keep in the fridge for 1 week. Macros for the sauce, per ½ tablespoon (7 ml): 53 Calories, 6 g Fat, 0 g Carbs, 0 g Protein.

MAPLE BACON DONUTS

MAKES: 6 donuts

1 DONUT: 263 Calories, 23 g Fat, 2 g Carbs, 12 g Protein

||||||||||||||||||||||||||||||||||||||||||||||

DONUTS

⅓ cup (80 g) butter, melted

2 tbsp (30 ml) heavy whipping cream

6 tbsp (42 g) brown sugar replacement (I recommend Swerve) or erythritol

4 eggs

2 tsp (10 ml) vanilla extract

1 cup (104 g) almond flour

1 tsp baking powder

GLAZE

2 tbsp (30 g) butter, melted

½ tsp maple extract

¼ to ½ cup (30 to 60 g) powdered erythritol

2 to 3 tbsp (30 to 45 ml) unsweetened almond milk, plus more as needed

5 strips thick-cut bacon, cooked until crisp, chopped

2 tbsp (15 g) brown sugar replacement (I recommend Swerve) or erythritol

Gone are the days of staring longingly into the glass case at your local bakery at the delicious, freshly baked donuts covered in all the good stuff! Now you can savor deliciously sweet and salty Maple Bacon Donuts—with the most perfect maple glaze—and not have to worry about an awful sugar crash. This cake-like donut will be giving you all the feels.

Preheat the oven to 350°F (176°C). Grease a donut pan.

To make the donuts, in a medium bowl, use a hand mixer to blend the butter, cream and sugar replacement until smooth. Add the eggs and vanilla and blend until combined. Add the almond flour and baking powder and mix well. Divide the batter into six portions and spoon the batter into the donut pan. A cupcake/muffin pan can be substituted if needed.

Bake for 15 to 18 minutes, or until lightly browned. Let cool for at least 10 minutes.

While the donuts are cooling, prepare the glaze. Combine the butter, maple extract and erythritol. Slowly add the almond milk and whisk until you create a smooth glaze—you may need to add a bit more almond milk if you desire a thinner glaze. Dip each donut in the glaze and sprinkle with bacon and a little of the sugar replacement.

||||||||||||||||||||||||||||||||||||||||||||||||||||||||||||||||||||||||||||||

TIP: Vanilla extract can be substituted for maple extract in the glaze if preferred.

MAPLE NUT FAUX-TMEAL

MAKES: 1 bowl

1 BOWL: 225 Calories, 18 g Fat,
3 g Carbs, 7 g Protein

||||||||||||||||||||||||||||||||||||||||||||||||

1 tbsp (10 g) chia seeds, ground

1 tbsp (7 g) ground flaxseed

2 tbsp (11 g) unsweetened
shredded coconut

½ tbsp (8 g) hemp hearts

1 tbsp (15 g) walnuts, diced

¼ tsp cinnamon

½ tsp maple extract

1 tbsp (7 g) brown sugar
replacement (I recommend Swerve)
or erythritol

½ cup (120 ml) unsweetened
almond milk

One of my fondest memories from a family trip to Scotland was sitting outside enjoying a warm bowl of oatmeal and taking in the beautiful scenery. And while I am not in Scotland anymore—and my carb count is MUCH lower these days—I was still missing that hearty breakfast to start my day. This Maple Nut Faux-tmeal warms the soul and keeps you full all morning long.

Simply combine the chia seeds, flaxseed, coconut, hemp hearts, walnuts, cinnamon, maple extract, sugar replacement and almond milk in a small, microwave-safe bowl. Cook in the microwave until it is smooth and piping hot, 60 to 90 seconds.

DOUBLE CHOCOLATE MUFFINS

MAKES: 10 muffins

1 MUFFIN: 188 Calories, 17 g Fat, 3 g Carbs, 5 g Protein

||||||||||||||||||||||||||||||||||||||||||||||||

1¼ cups (130 g) almond flour

¾ cup (90 g) powdered erythritol

2 tbsp (15 g) ground flaxseed

½ cup (40 g) unsweetened cocoa powder

2 tsp (9 g) baking powder

½ tsp ground cinnamon

5 tbsp (75 g) butter, melted

1 tsp vanilla extract

½ cup (120 ml) unsweetened almond milk

¼ cup (60 ml) sour cream

2 eggs

½ cup (85 g) sugar-free chocolate chips or 70%+ dark chocolate, chopped

Chocolate isn't just for dessert! As an adult you can absolutely indulge in these decadent desserts—I mean, muffins for breakfast, because what better way to be an adult than by eating dessert first?

Preheat the oven to 350°F (176°C). Line a muffin tin with ten liners and set aside.

In a large bowl, mix together the almond flour, erythritol, flaxseed, cocoa powder, baking powder and cinnamon. Stir the butter, vanilla, almond milk and sour cream into the almond flour mixture.

Add the eggs to the mixture and stir gently until fully combined. Fold in the chocolate.

Fill the muffin tins one-half to three-quarters full. You can also weigh the batter on a food scale and divide by ten to get the exact weight of batter per cup.

Bake for 20 minutes, or until a toothpick comes out clean. Let cool for at least 30 minutes—an hour or more if possible—to allow them to firm up. Store in the fridge for up to 5 days or in the freezer for up to a month.

BREAKFAST FAUX-GRANOLA BARS

MAKES: 15 bars

1 BAR: 343 Calories, 29 g Fat, 3 g Carbs, 9 g Protein

||||||||||||||||||||||||||||||||||||||||||||

2 cups (170 g) unsweetened coconut flakes, tightly packed

2 cups (220 g) slivered almonds

1½ cups (165 g) pecans, chopped

2 large eggs

½ cup (60 g) brown sugar replacement (I recommend Swerve) or erythritol

6 tbsp (95 g) sugar-free peanut butter

1 tsp vanilla extract

4 tbsp (60 ml) sugar-free pancake syrup

2 tbsp (30 g) coconut oil

½ cup (130 g) hemp hearts

1 tsp cinnamon

1 tsp salt

½ cup (85 g) sugar-free chocolate chips

These bars are great for those who just want to grab-and-go for breakfast—or a snack—and don't want to sacrifice taste. The Breakfast Faux-Granola Bars are packed with fiber to keep you full all morning. With a perfect mixture of sweet and crunchy, this Keto staple is mother-tested and kid-approved.

Preheat the oven to 375°F (190°C). Line an 8 x 13–inch (20 x 33–cm) pan with parchment paper.

Place the coconut flakes, almonds and pecans on individual baking sheets and bake until golden brown and toasted. The coconut flakes will take 2 to 4 minutes; the almonds, 3 to 5 minutes and the pecans, 7 to 10 minutes. Let cool completely.

Reduce the oven temperature to 350°F (176°C).

In a large bowl, whisk together the eggs and sugar replacement. In a small, microwave-safe bowl, melt the peanut butter, vanilla, syrup and coconut oil until smooth. This should take about 30 seconds. Whisk the peanut butter mixture into the egg mixture until well combined. Add in the coconut flakes, almonds, pecans, hemp hearts, cinnamon and salt. Fold in the chocolate chips.

Using damp hands or a nonstick spatula, press the mixture very firmly into the prepared pan. Bake for 17 minutes, or until just set. Let cool completely before cutting into bars.

LEMON POPPY DELIGHT MUFFINS

MAKES: 12 muffins

1 MUFFIN: 196 Calories, 16 g Fat, 3 g Carbs, 8 g Protein

||||||||||||||||||||||||||||||||||||||||||

MUFFINS

½ cup (120 ml) sour cream

4 large eggs

2 tsp (10 ml) vanilla extract

3 cups (312 g) almond flour

¾ cup (85 g) erythritol

2 tsp (9 g) baking powder

½ tsp cinnamon

¼ tsp salt

2 tbsp (20 g) poppy seeds

2 tbsp (30 ml) lemon juice

1 tbsp (10 g) lemon zest

LEMON GLAZE

¼ cup (30 g) powdered erythritol

¼ cup (60 ml) unsweetened almond milk

1 tsp lemon extract

I am a muffin person. I can't help but love the convenience of grabbing a pastry in the morning to pair with my tea, or running out the door and having something delicious to get my morning started. One of my favorite muffins has always been lemon poppy seed. It has a light and refreshing taste that reminds me of spring. When I am freezing during the cold winter months in New Hampshire, I make a batch of these bad Larrys and pretend the tulips are just blooming and warmer weather is on its way. This light and citrusy muffin, drizzled with a slightly tart glaze, will have you dreaming for that alarm clock to go off early for a taste of spring!

Preheat the oven to 325°F (162°C). Line a muffin tin with muffin liners.

To make the muffins, use a mixer to combine the sour cream, eggs and vanilla, blending for 30 seconds. Add the almond flour, erythritol, baking powder, cinnamon and salt, blending until smooth. If the batter is too thick, add ¼ cup (60 ml) of water to thin it out. Once the batter is smooth, mix in the poppy seeds, lemon juice and lemon zest.

Divide the mixture among the prepared muffin cups and bake for 25 to 30 minutes, or until just golden brown and firm to the touch. Allow to cool completely.

While the muffins are cooling, make the lemon glaze by combining the powdered erythritol, almond milk and lemon extract. Drizzle the glaze over the tops of the muffins.

BURRITO BREAKFAST BOWL

MAKES: 1 bowl

1 BOWL: 263 Calories, 21 g Fat,
3 g Carbs, 13 g Protein

||||||||||||||||||||||||||||||||||||||||||||||||

2 strips bacon

1 large egg

½ cup (50 g) cauliflower rice

1 tbsp (15 g) butter

1 cup (30 g) spinach, chopped small

¼ tsp chili pepper

¼ tsp ground cumin

¼ tsp garlic powder

¼ tsp onion powder

¼ tsp paprika

I have found cauliflower rice bowls to be a secret weapon to help hit your macros each day, because they are so customizable. If you find you need more fats, you can easily add avocado, sour cream or a drizzle of olive oil. If you need protein, you can add meat or eggs. They are loaded with flavor and light on the carbs! This is a breakfast bowl that packs flavor and will keep you full all morning.

In a nonstick pan, fry the bacon until crisp. Remove from the pan—leaving the bacon grease—and crumble into a bowl. Cook the egg in the grease to your liking. I prefer over easy, but cook to your preference. Add the egg to the bowl with the bacon.

In the same pan, add the cauliflower rice and sauté for 2 minutes. Add the butter, spinach, chili pepper, cumin, garlic powder, onion powder and paprika. Cook over medium-high heat for 2 minutes. Add the sautéed mixture to the bacon and egg bowl, mixing to combine.

GOOD OLD-FASHIONED PANCAKES

MAKES: 12 pancakes

1 PANCAKE: 102 Calories, 7 g Fat, 1 g Carbs, 6 g Protein

||||||||||||||||||||||||||||||||||||||||||||

1 cup (104 g) almond flour

¼ cup (26 g) coconut flour

2 tbsp (15 g) erythritol

1 tsp baking powder

6 large eggs

6 tbsp (90 ml) unsweetened almond milk

1 tsp vanilla extract

No need to pass on Saturday morning stacks! With this simple, gluten-free, Keto pancake recipe, you only need a few ingredients and you might even have your non-Keto friends hopping on the Keto train! Fluffy and soft, they are perfect for drizzling with sugar-free syrup or making a breakfast sandwich—watch out, McGriddle!

In a large bowl, combine the almond flour, coconut flour, erythritol and baking powder. In a separate bowl, combine the eggs, almond milk and vanilla. Slowly mix the wet ingredients with the dry ingredients.

Pour ¼ cup (28 g) of the batter onto a greased griddle, cooking on medium-low for 1 minute per side. If you would like smaller pancakes, make two pancakes per ¼ cup (28 g) of the batter.

CREAMY PEANUT BUTTER BANANA CHOCOLATE FRAPPE

MAKES: 1 frappe

1 FRAPPE: 289 Calories, 24 g Fat, 6 g Carbs, 10 g Protein

||||||||||||||||||||||||||||||||||||||||||||||||||

2 tbsp (11 g) unsweetened cocoa powder

1 tbsp (7 g) powdered erythritol

1 tbsp (15 g) sugar-free peanut butter

10 oz (300 ml) unsweetened almond milk

½ avocado

½ tsp banana extract

1½ cups (45 g) spinach, optional

1 cup (145 g) ice

If you aren't from New England, you may refer to these as "shakes." But no matter what you call them, this Creamy Peanut Butter Banana Chocolate Frappe is bananas and perfect for a sweet grab-and-go breakfast. Packed with some healthy fats, protein and CHOCOLATE, how can you go wrong?!

Simply combine the cocoa powder, erythritol, peanut butter, almond milk, avocado, banana extract, spinach, if using, and ice in a blender, and blend until smooth, about 1 minute.

PUMPKIN MAPLE-GLAZED DONUTS

MAKES: 12 donuts

1 DONUT: 298 Calories, 28 g Fat, 3 g Carbs, 9 g Protein

||||||||||||||||||||||||||||||||||||||||||||||

DONUTS

⅔ cup (160 g) butter, melted

¼ cup (60 g) pumpkin puree

½ cup (60 g) erythritol

8 medium eggs

2 tsp (10 ml) vanilla extract

2 cups (208 g) almond flour

2 tsp (9 g) baking powder

2 tsp (5 g) cinnamon

2 tsp (5 g) pumpkin pie seasoning

¼ tsp ground cloves

GLAZE

½ cup (60 g) powdered erythritol

1½ tbsp (22 g) butter

4 oz (120 g) cream cheese, softened

2 tbsp (30 ml) heavy cream

1 tsp maple extract

New England may have the LONGEST winters ever, it seems, but we do know how to do fall right! And one of my favorite fall traditions has always been pumpkin donuts. And with cutting carbs and sugar I once thought that this tradition was over. But where there is a will, there is a way! These are the BEST fall donuts. Soft, cake-like and smothered in a warm maple glaze, this donut is perfect for that cool fall morning—and you won't even bat an eye at those 3 grams of carbs!

Preheat the oven to 350°F (176°C). Grease a donut pan.

Using a hand mixer, blend the butter, pumpkin and erythritol in a medium bowl until smooth. Add the eggs and vanilla and blend until combined. Add the almond flour, baking powder, cinnamon, pumpkin pie seasoning and cloves and mix well.

Spoon the dough into the donut pan. A muffin pan can be substituted if needed. Bake for 15 to 18 minutes, or until lightly browned. Let cool.

Prepare the glaze while the donuts are cooling. In a small, microwavable bowl, mix the powdered erythritol, butter, cream cheese, heavy cream and maple extract and microwave for 30 seconds.

Dunk the tops of the donuts into the glaze. If the glaze is too thick, add almond milk ½ teaspoon at a time until you reach your desired consistency and heat for an additional 30 seconds; if it's too thin, add more erythritol ¼ teaspoon at a time until you reach your desired consistency. The donuts can be kept in the fridge or the freezer.

MEAN GREEN SMOOTHIE

MAKES: 1 smoothie

1 SMOOTHIE: 218 Calories,
15 g Fat, 6 g Carbs, 5 g Protein

||||||||||||||||||||||||||||||||||||||||||||||||||||||||||

¼ cup (36 g) frozen strawberries

½ cup (62 g) frozen raspberries

½ avocado

1 cup (30 g) spinach

10 oz (300 ml) unsweetened
almond milk

½ tsp vanilla extract

1 to 2 tbsp (7 to 15 g) powdered
erythritol

I often hear "I could never do Keto, because you can't have any fruit." But you absolutely can still have berries, in moderation. And this Mean Green Smoothie is just as good as the smoothies that have much more fruit in them, and with only a tenth of the sugar. There is quite a bit of fiber in here to keep you full, and without that blood glucose spike and drop associated with the higher sugar smoothies, you won't be looking for another meal as soon as you are done. And the best part—it's pretty dang tasty!

Combine the strawberries, raspberries, avocado, spinach, almond milk, vanilla and erythritol in a blender and blend until smooth and creamy.

CHOCOLATE LOVER'S BULLETPROOF HOT COCOA

MAKES: 1 serving

1 SERVING: 222 Calories, 19 g Fat, 4 g Carbs, 2 g Protein

||||||||||||||||||||||||||||||||||||||||||||||||

10 oz (300 ml) unsweetened almond milk, hot

1 tbsp (15 g) butter

2½ tbsp (12 g) unsweetened cocoa powder

2½ tbsp (22 g) powdered erythritol

1 tbsp (10 g) sugar-free, low-carb chocolate chips

½ tsp vanilla extract

Pinch of salt

While we will never give up our coffee, some mornings call for something a bit more decadent. Indulge in a sinfully delicious chocolate beverage that warms you right through! Creamy, chocolaty and surprisingly filling, this hot cocoa will get your morning moving.

Simply blend the almond milk, butter, cocoa powder, erythritol, chocolate chips, vanilla and salt until frothy. Pour and enjoy!

||||||||||||||||||||||||||||||||||||||||||||||||||||||||||||||||||||||||||||||||||||||||||||||

TIPS: If you still need to have your coffee, substitute coffee for the almond milk to make more of a mocha.

To make the hot cocoa dairy-free, substitute coconut oil for the butter and use vegan chocolate.

COFFEE CAKE SWIRL MUFFINS

MAKES: 12 muffins

1 MUFFIN: 234 Calories, 20 g Fat, 3 g Carbs, 7 g Protein

||||||||||||||||||||||||||||||||||||||||||||||||||

MUFFINS

2 tbsp (30 g) butter, room temperature

2 oz (60 g) cream cheese, room temperature

⅔ cup (80 g) powdered erythritol

4 eggs, room temperature

1 tsp vanilla extract

½ cup (120 ml) unsweetened almond milk

1 cup (104 g) almond flour

½ cup (52 g) coconut flour

1 tsp baking powder

½ tsp cinnamon

¼ tsp salt

STREUSEL TOPPING

1 cup (104 g) almond flour

2 tbsp (13 g) coconut flour

½ cup (60 g) powdered erythritol

¼ cup (60 g) butter, softened

2 tsp (5 g) cinnamon

On the mornings you have time to sit down with a cup of coffee, this is a muffin made for dunking! Topped with a crumbly, buttery streusel topping, these coffee cake muffins are delicious and a beginner baker's dream! Simple, flavorful and everything you want out of a low-carb pastry.

Preheat the oven to 350°F (176°C). Line a standard muffin tin with paper liners.

To make the muffins, in a food processor, combine the butter, cream cheese, erythritol, eggs, vanilla, almond milk, almond flour, coconut flour, baking powder, cinnamon and salt. Mix thoroughly. Divide the dough between the prepared muffin tins.

To prepare the streusel topping, combine the almond flour, coconut flour, erythritol, butter and cinnamon in a food processor and pulse until crumbs form. Sprinkle on top of the batter.

Bake for 20 to 25 minutes, or until a toothpick comes out clean.

||||||||||||||||||||||||||||||||||||||||||||||||||||||||||||||||||||||||||

TIP: The muffins are best stored in the fridge for up to 5 days, but they can be left out for a day in an airtight container.

EVERYTHING BAGELS

MAKES: 9 bagels

1 BAGEL: 329 Calories, 26 g Fat, 3 g Carbs, 18 g Protein

||||||||||||||||||||||||||||||||||||||||||||

BAGELS
2 cups (208 g) almond flour

1 tbsp (14 g) baking powder

1 tsp garlic powder

2 tbsp (15 g) erythritol

3 large eggs, divided

3 cups (336 g) low-moisture mozzarella cheese, shredded

5 oz (150 g) cream cheese

TOPPING
2 tsp (7 g) white sesame seeds

1½ tsp (5 g) black sesame seeds

1½ tsp (5 g) dried onion

1 tsp salt

½ tsp poppy seeds

While my friends from New Jersey and New York may have cornered the bagel market, these bagels won't disappoint if you are craving that fresh bakery-style bagel. Delicious, low-carb bagels perfect for not only breakfast, but to use in place of buns or bread to make your favorite sandwich! Hello BLT on an everything bagel.

Preheat the oven to 425°F (218°C). Line a rimmed baking sheet with parchment paper.

In a medium mixing bowl, combine the almond flour, baking powder, garlic powder and erythritol, mixing until well combined. In a separate small bowl, crack 1 egg and whisk with a fork to make an egg wash. Set aside.

In a large, microwave-safe bowl, combine the mozzarella and cream cheese and microwave for 90 seconds. Stir to combine, and microwave for an additional minute. Mix until well combined. Add the remaining 2 eggs and the almond flour mixture to the bowl with the cheese. Mix until all the ingredients are well incorporated. If the dough gets too stringy and is unworkable, microwave for 30 seconds and continue mixing.

Divide the dough into nine equal portions, rolling each portion into a ball. Gently press your finger into the center of each dough ball to form a ring, and stretch the ring to make a small hole in the center to form it into a bagel shape.

Bake on the middle rack for 12 to 14 minutes, or until golden brown.

Make the topping by combining the sesame seeds, onion, salt and poppy seeds. Brush the top of each bagel with the egg wash, sprinkle with the topping and bake for an additional 1 to 2 minutes.

||||||||||||||||||||||||||||||||||||||||||||||||||||

TIP: You can use 3 tablespoons (22 g) of store-bought everything bagel seasoning instead of making it yourself.

Oh Kale Yeah,
IT'S LUNCH!

Ditch the sandwich and drive-thru, and start looking forward to lunch again! The endless options found in this chapter will not only keep you satiated, but will also take your taste buds on an international journey— no passport required! From Spanakopita (page 69) and Jalapeño Popper Soup (page 59) to a Summer Antipasto Salad (page 63), lunch will be anything but boring!

THE BEST MAC AND CHEESE

MAKES: 6 servings

1 SERVING: 307 Calories, 25 g Fat, 7 g Carbs, 12 g Protein

||||||||||||||||||||||||||||||||||||||||||||

18 oz (510 g) fresh cauliflower florets, steamed

12 oz (340 g) cauliflower rice, steamed

4 cups (452 g) Cheddar cheese

½ cup (120 ml) heavy cream

1 cup (240 ml) chicken broth

4 oz (120 g) cream cheese

1¼ tsp (3 g) ground mustard

1 tsp parsley

1 to 2 tsp (5 g) garlic powder

1 tsp onion powder

¼ tsp dill weed

¼ tsp chives

¼ tsp salt

¼ tsp black pepper

The words *best*, *amazing* and *incredible* get tossed around all the time. But this recipe is truly deserving of its title. Creamy and flavorful with no cauliflower taste, you won't even notice the pasta is missing.

Place the cauliflower florets, cauliflower rice, Cheddar cheese, cream, broth, cream cheese, mustard, parsley, garlic powder, onion powder, dill weed, chives, salt and black pepper in a slow cooker. Mix well and cook on low for 3 hours, stirring occasionally. Alternatively, you can bake in the oven at 350°F (176°C) for 35 to 40 minutes.

||||||||||||||||||||||||||||||||||||||||||||||||||||||||||||||||||||||||||||||||||||||||||||||||||

TIP: If you have the macros available, add in bacon or pulled pork.

CREAMY TOMATO SOUP

MAKES: 5 servings

1 SERVING: 336 Calories, 31 g Fat, 6 g Carbs, 5 g Protein

||||||||||||||||||||||||||||||||||||||||||||

½ cup (120 g) butter

4 cloves garlic, minced

1 (20-oz [560-g]) can diced tomatoes, with liquid

2 cups (480 ml) chicken broth

½ cup (120 ml) heavy cream

4 oz (120 g) cream cheese

1 tbsp (7 g) erythritol

1 tsp basil

½ tsp red pepper flakes

½ tsp oregano

½ tsp salt

½ tsp black pepper

This is one of the most LOVED recipes I have ever made. It's the tomato soup recipe that will change your life. No exaggeration. It has had tomato soup haters proclaiming their love for it after just one bowl.

Melt the butter in a large pot over medium-high heat. Once the butter has melted, add the garlic and sauté for 1 minute, stirring occasionally. Add the tomatoes, broth, cream, cream cheese, erythritol, basil, red pepper flakes, oregano, salt and black pepper. Bring to a boil, then use an immersion blender or blender to puree the soup. Simmer for 5 minutes after blended.

|||||||||||||||||||||||||||||||||||||||||||||||||||||||||||||||||||||||||||||||||||||||||||

TIPS: The soup can be frozen for 1 to 2 months. I like to portion it into single servings and freeze in zip top bags for faster thawing.

To make this dairy-free, substitute coconut milk and olive oil for the cream cheese and heavy cream, and use dairy-free butter.

To make this vegetarian, substitute vegetable broth for the chicken broth.

BLT BOWL

MAKES: 4 servings

1 SERVING: 444 Calories, 41 g Fat, 6 g Carbs, 13 g Protein

||||||||||||||||||||||||||||||||||||||||||||||||||

DRESSING

½ cup (120 ml) mayo

¼ cup (60 ml) sour cream

2 tbsp (30 ml) unsweetened almond milk

½ tsp black pepper

¼ tsp salt

¼ tsp garlic powder

¼ tsp chili flakes

½ tsp paprika

2 tsp (3 g) parsley

1 tsp onion powder

1 tsp white distilled vinegar

BOWL

10 oz (280 g) romaine lettuce, chopped

12 oz (340 g) cauliflower rice, steamed

1 cup (200 g) Roma tomatoes, diced

1 cup (113 g) Cheddar cheese, shredded

8 strips bacon, cooked and chopped

Everyone's favorite sandwich—hold the bread, but not the flavor! Who doesn't love a good BLT? So, I thought, let's kick this up a notch. Turn it into a combination of a "rice" bowl and salad to really satisfy even those with big appetites to help get through the lunch munchies. Full of bacon, veggies and a finger-licking-good dressing, I am sure you will love this one as much as I do.

To prepare the dressing, combine the mayo, sour cream, almond milk, black pepper, salt, garlic powder, chili flakes, paprika, parsley, onion powder and vinegar. Stir until smooth and well combined. Set aside.

To make the bowls, combine the lettuce, cauliflower rice, tomatoes, cheese and bacon. Toss with the dressing until well combined.

JALAPEÑO POPPER SOUP

MAKES: 4 servings

1 SERVING: 259 Calories, 22 g Fat, 6 g Carbs, 10 g Protein

|||||||||||||||||||||||||||||||||||||||||||

4 oz (120 g) cream cheese

1 cup (113 g) Cheddar cheese

3¼ cups (780 ml) chicken broth

1 tbsp (15 g) butter

8 oz (225 g) cauliflower florets, steamed

4 jalapeños, seeded and diced

1 tsp parsley

½ tsp dill weed

1 tsp freeze-dried chives

1 tsp onion powder

¼ tsp salt

¼ tsp black pepper

5 strips bacon, cooked and chopped

¼ tsp xanthan gum

Everyone's favorite appetizer is ready to take on your lunchtime cravings! This soup is one of the most popular recipes I have ever made, and I ALWAYS need to allot for two servings, because one simply isn't enough!

In a medium pot set over medium-high heat, combine the cream cheese, Cheddar cheese, chicken broth and butter. Stir until smooth. Add the cauliflower and puree with an immersion blender. Add the jalapeños, parsley, dill, chives, onion powder, salt, black pepper, bacon and xanthan gum. Simmer for 5 to 10 minutes.

BROCCOLI SALAD 2.0

MAKES: 8 servings

1 SERVING: 291 Calories, 27 g Fat, 5 g Carbs, 7 g Protein

||||||||||||||||||||||||||||||||||||||||||||||

SALAD

6 cups (432 g) fresh broccoli florets

10 oz (280 g) shredded cabbage

1 cup (113 g) sharp Cheddar cheese, shredded

6 strips bacon, cooked and crumbled (you should have about ½ cup [60 g])

¼ cup (40 g) red onion, diced

DRESSING

¾ cup (180 ml) mayo

½ cup (120 ml) sour cream

3 tbsp (45 ml) white vinegar

¼ cup (30 g) erythritol

¼ tsp salt

¼ tsp black pepper

2 tsp (10 ml) yellow mustard

¼ tsp ground mustard

Warning: This may be one of the MOST delicious salads you ever make! In fact, it is routinely requested—if not outright demanded—by friends and family at all our summer BBQs! Break away from your average lunch salad and make this crisp and flavorful broccoli salad.

To make the salad, combine the broccoli, cabbage, Cheddar cheese, bacon and onion in a large bowl.

To prepare the dressing, in a small bowl, whisk the mayo, sour cream, vinegar, erythritol, salt, black pepper, yellow mustard and ground mustard until smooth and well combined. Pour the dressing over the salad and stir well. Refrigerate for at least 1 hour before serving.

||||||||||||||||||||||||||||||||||||||||||||||||||||||||||||||||||||||||||||||||||||||||

TIP: To ensure the salad is crisp, do not use frozen broccoli in place of the fresh broccoli.

SUMMER ANTIPASTO SALAD

MAKES: 5 servings

1 SERVING: 319 Calories, 28 g Fat, 4 g Carbs, 13 g Protein

||||||||||||||||||||||||||||||||||||||||||||||||||

DRESSING

¼ cup (60 ml) extra-virgin olive oil

2 tbsp (30 ml) white wine vinegar

1 tbsp (15 ml) water

½ tsp erythritol

1 tsp freshly squeezed lemon juice

3 tbsp (22 g) freshly grated Parmesan cheese

½ tsp garlic powder

½ tsp parsley

½ tsp basil

⅛ tsp oregano

Pinch of red pepper flakes

SALAD

12 oz (340 g) cauliflower florets, steamed

½ cup (75 g) red bell pepper, chopped

½ cup (75 g) green bell pepper, chopped

2 oz (60 g) pepperoni

3 oz (85 g) black olives

3 oz (85 g) green olives

2 oz (60 g) canned artichoke hearts, diced

4 oz (120 g) pepperoncini peppers, diced

¼ lb (120 g) mozzarella cheese, diced

A flavorful and colorful Italian staple, this is the perfect salad to bring along on a picnic or enjoy with a glass of wine. The vegetables pair perfectly with a traditional Italian dressing. It will win over the hearts of even the most adamant cauliflower haters.

To prepare the dressing, in a large bowl, combine the olive oil, vinegar, water, erythritol, lemon juice, Parmesan, garlic powder, parsley, basil, oregano and red pepper flakes.

To make the salad, combine the cauliflower, bell peppers, pepperoni, olives, artichoke hearts, pepperoncini peppers and mozzarella. Add the salad dressing and coat well. Refrigerate for at least 1 hour before serving—overnight is ideal.

CHINESE-STYLE FRIED RICE

MAKES: 1 serving

1 SERVING: 383 Calories, 35 g Fat, 6 g Carbs, 11 g Protein

||||||||||||||||||||||||||||||||||||||||||||||||||

2 tbsp (30 g) butter

1½ cups (150 g) cauliflower rice

1 egg

2 tbsp (30 ml) soy sauce

½ tsp garlic powder

¼ tsp ground ginger

½ tbsp (8 ml) white vinegar

½ tbsp (8 ml) sesame oil

½ tbsp (8 g) chili paste, optional

Who needs takeout when you can whip up your own Chinese fried rice? Traditionally seasoned and deliciously filling, it's the lunch bowl that you can't help but make over and over again.

In a medium skillet set over medium-high heat, melt the butter. Add the cauliflower rice to the butter and sauté until the rice is tender, about 6 to 7 minutes. Push the rice to the side and crack the egg in the pan, scramble with a spatula, then mix in with the cauliflower rice once the egg has cooked. Add the soy sauce, garlic powder, ginger, white vinegar, sesame oil and chili paste, if using, and mix well. Reduce the heat to low, cover the pan and cook for 5 minutes.

PAELLA BOWLS

MAKES: 5 servings

1 SERVING: 155 Calories, 10 g Fat, 6 g Carbs, 4 g Protein

||||||||||||||||||||||||||||||||||||||||||||||||||

3 tbsp (45 ml) extra-virgin olive oil

¼ cup (40 g) yellow onion, diced

1½ tsp (7 g) salt, divided

5 cloves garlic, minced

2 tsp (4 g) paprika

1 (10-oz [280-g]) can diced tomatoes, drained

4 cups (400 g) cauliflower rice, steamed

1 cup (240 ml) chicken broth

½ tsp turmeric

1 cup (150 g) red bell pepper, diced

¼ cup (60 g) green olives

2 tbsp (30 ml) lemon juice

¼ cup (38 g) green beans, chopped

Growing up with a family from Spain meant that paella was as much a childhood staple as peanut butter and jelly. This bowl is vibrant in color—thanks to the turmeric—and full to the brim with traditionally seasoned "rice." These bowls are a delicious, healthy take on the Spanish rice dish, full of flavor and lacking only in carbs.

Heat the olive oil in a large skillet over medium-high heat. Add the onion and a pinch of salt, cooking until the onion is tender and translucent, about 3 minutes. Stir in the garlic and paprika and cook for 30 seconds. Add the tomatoes and cook until the mixture begins to thicken slightly, about 2 minutes. Stir in the cauliflower rice and cook for 1 minute. Add the broth, turmeric and remaining salt. Stir well. Add the bell pepper, green olives, lemon juice and green beans. Cover and cook on low heat for 15 minutes.

|||||||||||||||||||||||||||||||||||||||||||||||||||||||||||||||||||||||||||||||||||

TIPS: If you are in need of more protein, you can easily add shredded chicken or ground beef.

If you need more fat, a little dollop of sour cream, avocado or olive oil drizzled over the top would be great!

BRUSSELS WITH AIOLI

MAKES: 4 servings

1 SERVING: 227 Calories, 21 g Fat,
6 g Carbs, 4 g Protein

||||||||||||||||||||||||||||||||||||||||||||||

BRUSSELS SPROUTS

1 lb (454 g) Brussels sprouts, halved

3 tbsp (45 g) butter, melted

1 tsp garlic powder

½ tsp salt

¼ tsp black pepper

AIOLI

¼ cup (60 ml) mayo

2 tbsp (30 ml) lemon juice

1 tsp powdered erythritol

1 tbsp (15 g) chili paste

½ tsp garlic powder

½ tsp salt

Crisp on the outside and tender on the inside, these Brussels sprouts are pure perfection! Drizzled with a creamy aioli that's both sweet and a bit spicy, your taste buds will be in heaven.

Preheat the oven to 450°F (232°C). Line a baking sheet with aluminum foil.

Place the Brussels sprouts in a large bowl and add the butter, garlic powder, salt and black pepper. Place the Brussels sprouts on the lined baking sheet, and bake for 20 minutes, or until crispy.

While the Brussels sprouts are baking, prepare the aioli. Whisk the mayo, lemon juice, erythritol, chili paste, garlic powder and salt until smooth.

Drizzle the aioli over the sprouts.

*See image on page 52.

SPANAKOPITA

MAKES: 8 servings

1 SERVING: 275 Calories, 23 g Fat, 5 g Carbs, 18 g Protein

||||||||||||||||||||||||||||||||||||||||||||||||

DOUGH

2 cups (224 g) mozzarella cheese

2 oz (60 g) cream cheese

1 cup (104 g) almond flour

½ cup (52 g) coconut flour

1 egg

1 tsp baking powder

½ tsp salt

FILLING

1 egg

10 cups (300 g) fresh spinach, chopped small

4 oz (120 g) feta cheese, crumbled

2 tbsp (7 g) parsley

1 tsp dried dill

¼ tsp nutmeg

½ tsp erythritol

½ tsp onion powder

¾ tsp garlic powder

Pinch of salt

Spanakopita is a crispy, authentic Greek spinach-stuffed pastry bursting with flavor. The balance of feta and traditional spices will have you shouting *Opa!*

Preheat the oven to 375°F (190°C). Line a baking sheet with parchment paper.

To make the dough, in a microwave-safe bowl, combine the mozzarella and cream cheese and microwave for 1 minute. Stir and cook for an additional 45 seconds. Stir well and add the almond flour, coconut flour, egg, baking powder and salt. With damp hands, mix well. The dough will be very sticky—you may need to microwave for an additional 30 seconds if it is too stringy and difficult to work with.

To make the filling, separate the egg yolk from the egg white, and set the yolk aside. Mix the egg white with the spinach, feta, parsley, dill, nutmeg, erythritol, onion powder, garlic powder and salt.

Roll the dough between two pieces of parchment paper into a 6 x 18–inch (15 x 45–cm) rectangle, or as close as you can get. Remove the top piece of parchment, and cut the dough in half lengthwise with a pizza cutter or knife. Put the filling in the center of one piece, leaving a 1-inch (2.5-cm) border, then top with the other piece of dough. Cut into 8 equal pieces.

Place the dough onto the baking sheet and gently press the edges together with your thumb and index finger. Make a few small slits in the top of the dough with a small knife. Brush with the egg yolk.

Bake the spanakopita for 30 minutes, or until golden brown. Make sure not to overbake, as the crust will harden as it cools.

||||||||||||||||||||||||||||||||||||||||||||||||||||||||||||||||||||||||||||||||||||

TIPS: Personally, I love garlic, so I use 1 to 1½ teaspoons (3 to 4 g) in the filling!

These freeze well. Just reheat in the microwave, air fryer or oven.

STRAWBERRY BLISS SALAD

MAKES: 1 salad

1 SALAD: 263 Calories, 24 g Fat, 5 g Carbs, 8 g Protein

||||||||||||||||||||||||||||||||||||||||||||||

DRESSING

¼ cup (60 ml) mayo

¼ cup (60 ml) extra-virgin olive oil

3 tbsp (45 ml) unsweetened almond milk

4 medium strawberries

1 tbsp (15 ml) white vinegar

1 tbsp (15 ml) lemon juice

¼ tsp salt

1 tbsp (10 g) poppy seeds

SALAD

1 cup (75 g) romaine lettuce, chopped

3 cups (90 g) spinach, chopped

¼ cup (50 g) tomatoes, diced

2 tbsp (30 g) walnuts, chopped

2 tbsp (19 g) feta cheese

This homemade strawberry dressing is the perfect balance of sweet and tart. Drizzled over a bed of greens with feta and walnuts, you will think you just ordered it from a local bistro!

To make the dressing, combine the mayo, olive oil, almond milk, strawberries, vinegar, lemon juice and salt in a food processor and blend until smooth. Stir in the poppy seeds. Refrigerate until ready to use.

To make the salad, toss the lettuce, spinach, tomatoes, walnuts and feta with 2 tablespoons (30 ml) of the dressing. You can use more if you have the macros available.

||||||||||||||||||||||||||||||||||||||||||||||||||||||||||||||||||||||||||

TIPS: The dressing recipe yields enough for approximately 8 servings.

You can always use a different dressing if you like! The individual macros for 2 tablespoons (30 ml) of the dressing are: 119 Calories, 14 g Fat, 1 g Carbs, 0 g Protein.

The salad will keep in the fridge for up to a week. To prevent the lettuce and spinach from getting soggy, do not dress the salad before storing. Store the dressing in a separate container and dress the salad just before eating.

VEGGIE MINESTRONE SOUP

MAKES: 6 servings

1 SERVING: 158 Calories, 9 g Fat, 6 g Carbs, 6 g Protein

||||||||||||||||||||||||||||||||||||||||||||||||||

4 tbsp (60 ml) extra-virgin olive oil

¼ cup (40 g) yellow onion, chopped

2 celery ribs, chopped

½ cup (62 g) zucchini, chopped

6 oz (170 g) radishes, quartered

1 cup (100 g) cauliflower rice

4 cloves garlic, minced

¼ cup (60 g) tomato paste

½ tsp oregano

½ tsp thyme

1 (10-oz [280-g]) can diced tomatoes, with liquid

4 cups (960 ml) chicken broth

1 cup (240 ml) water

1 tsp salt

½ tsp red pepper flakes

½ tsp black pepper

2 cups (60 g) spinach

1 tbsp (15 ml) lemon juice

Filled to the brim with nutritious vegetables and an irresistible flavor, this hearty Italian soup is also incredibly easy to make. A warm bowl on a brisk afternoon will warm you right up.

In a stock pot or Dutch oven, heat the olive oil over medium-high heat. Add the onion, celery, zucchini, radishes and cauliflower rice and sauté for 5 minutes. Add the garlic, tomato paste, oregano, thyme, canned tomatoes, broth, water, salt, red pepper flakes, black pepper, spinach and lemon juice and stir well. Reduce the heat to medium-low and cook for 30 minutes, stirring occasionally.

||||||||||||||||||||||||||||||||||||||||||||||||||||||||||||||||||||||||||||||||||

TIPS: If you are in need of more protein, you can easily add shredded chicken or ground beef.

If you need more fat, a little dollop of sour cream mixed in is AMAZING!

COBB SALAD 2.0

MAKES: 1 serving

1 SERVING: 429 Calories, 37 g Fat, 6 g Carbs, 16 g Protein

||||||||||||||||||||||||||||||||||||||||||||||||||

DRESSING

½ cup (120 ml) mayo

½ cup (120 ml) sour cream

½ cup (120 ml) half and half

¾ tsp dill weed

½ tsp parsley

½ tsp chives

¼ tsp onion powder

½ tsp garlic powder

¼ tsp salt

⅛ tsp finely cracked black pepper

2 tsp (10 ml) white vinegar

SALAD

1 hardboiled egg, roughly chopped into small pieces

2 strips thick-cut bacon, cooked and crumbled

¼ medium avocado, diced

4 oz (120 g) romaine lettuce, chopped

4 oz (120 g) spinach, chopped

The cobb salad is the popular kid of the salad world. Topped with bacon, avocado and an egg, it's full of good fats and some of the most loved Keto-friendly foods. Being a self-proclaimed ranch hater, for years I had been eating my cobb salads with blue cheese dressing. Until this. I was working on a homemade ranch recipe for my husband to get him to give up the bottled brand with the S-word in it. I took a little taste and fell in love—it's creamy perfection that converted this ranch hater!

To prepare the dressing, combine the mayo, sour cream, half and half, dill, parsley, chives, onion powder, garlic powder, salt, black pepper and vinegar in a blender and blend on high for a full minute. Refrigerate until ready to serve.

Assemble the egg, bacon, avocado, lettuce and spinach in a bowl or plate and drizzle with 2 tablespoons (30 ml) of the dressing.

||||||||||||||||||||||||||||||||||||||||||||||||||||||||||||||||||||||||||||||

TIPS: This is a big salad! Sometimes I split it into two and have half in the early afternoon and the other half in the late afternoon.

If you need more protein, add some chicken.

You will have extra dressing. It stores well in an airtight container in the fridge for up to a week. The macros for 1 serving (2 tablespoons [30 ml]) are: 94 Calories, 10 g Fat, 1 g Carbs, 1 g Protein.

BACON AND SPINACH CALZONE

MAKES: 6 servings

1 SERVING: 238 Calories, 18 g Fat, 3 g Carbs, 13 g Protein

||||||||||||||||||||||||||||||||||||||||||||||

CRUST

1 cup (104 g) almond flour

3 tbsp (21 g) coconut flour

2 tsp (9 g) xanthan gum

1 tsp baking powder

¼ tsp salt

1 tsp Italian seasoning

½ tsp garlic powder

¼ tsp onion powder

2 tsp (10 ml) apple cider vinegar

2 tsp (10 ml) water

2 eggs, divided

FILLING

1 cup (112 g) mozzarella cheese, shredded

6 oz (170 g) spinach, chopped small

5 strips bacon, cooked and chopped

½ tsp garlic powder

½ tsp Italian seasoning

The Italian in me couldn't put together a cookbook and leave out a crusty calzone stuffed full of spinach and bacon goodness! As with most things in life, you can really make this your own! Adjust the filling ingredients to your tastes—add more veggies, or even some ground meat.

Preheat the oven to 400°F (204°C).

To make the crust, in a large bowl, whisk together the almond flour, coconut flour, xanthan gum, baking powder, salt, Italian seasoning, garlic powder and onion powder. In a separate small bowl, mix the apple cider vinegar, water and 1 egg. Combine with the flour mixture. With damp hands, knead the dough until all the ingredients are well mixed. Cover the bowl and refrigerate for 5 minutes.

Roll out a piece of parchment paper and place the dough on top. Layer a second piece on top and roll the dough out to 12 inches (30 cm) in diameter. Remove the top layer of parchment and spread the mozzarella cheese evenly over half of the dough. Top with the spinach and bacon. Sprinkle the garlic powder and Italian seasoning over the spinach and bacon. Fold the other half of the dough over the side with the toppings, pressing the edges down very firmly.

In a small bowl, beat the remaining egg and brush the calzone with the egg wash.

Place the calzone and the bottom piece of parchment paper on a baking sheet. Bake for 25 minutes or until the crust is crisp and golden. Allow to rest for 3 minutes before slicing.

||||||||||||||||||||||||||||||||||||||||||||||||||||||||||||||||||||||||||||||||

TIP: If you have extra macros, dip the calzone in marinara sauce or a little melted butter with minced garlic or garlic powder.

BBQ CAULIFLOWER RICE BOWL

MAKES: 1 serving

1 SERVING: 419 Calories, 38 g Fat,
2 g Carbs, 10 g Protein

||||||||||||||||||||||||||||||||||||||||||||||||

2 tbsp (30 g) butter, divided

1 egg

1½ cups (45 g) spinach

1 cup (100 g) cauliflower rice,
steamed

¼ tsp garlic powder

¼ tsp paprika

¼ tsp oregano

¼ tsp cayenne pepper

Salt and black pepper, to taste

½ avocado, diced

This is a flavorful take on a rice bowl—but without all the carbs. Full of good fats and veggies, this is a great alternative to a salad for when you still need the veggies but want to spice up your lunch.

In a medium saucepan, melt 1 tablespoon (15 g) of the butter. Once the butter is melted, scramble the egg in the pan. Move the egg to the side and add the remaining 1 tablespoon (15 g) of butter, spinach and cauliflower rice. Add the garlic powder, paprika, oregano, cayenne pepper, salt and black pepper and sauté until the spinach wilts, about 3 minutes, mixing the egg in with the other ingredients. Place everything in a bowl and top with the avocado.

ZUPPA TOSCANA

MAKES: 5 servings

1 SERVING: 333 Calories, 25 g Fat, 6 g Carbs, 19 g Protein

||||||||||||||||||||||||||||||||||||||||||||||||||

2 tbsp (30 g) butter

1 lb (454 g) ground pork

¼ cup (40 g) onion, chopped

1½ tbsp (5 g) Italian seasoning

1 tsp crushed red pepper

3 cloves garlic, minced

6 cups (1.5 L) chicken broth

1 lb (454 g) radishes, quartered

20 oz (560 g) fresh spinach, chopped

8.5 oz (250 ml) canned full-fat coconut milk

Salt and black pepper, to taste

This is a classic Zuppa Toscana soup—creamy, flavorful and warms you to the bone. Not only is this soup super simple to make, it's much better than the last time you had it at a chain restaurant. And healthier too!

In a large stock pot over medium-high heat, add the butter and pork. Cook for 5 to 7 minutes, or until browned. Add the onion, Italian seasoning and crushed red pepper and sauté for 3 minutes. Add the garlic and stir for 1 minute, then add the broth and radishes. Bring the soup to a boil then reduce the heat and simmer, covered, for 10 minutes. Add the spinach and coconut milk and simmer for 5 minutes, until the radishes can be easily pierced with a fork. Add salt and black pepper to taste. Serve immediately.

Winner, Winner
CHICKEN DINNER

Chicken dinner will NEVER be boring again! Put a delicious spin on your dinner routine—try out flavorful herb pairings that will knock your socks off! From the Bacon Chicken Caesar Casserole (page 84) to the Chicken Pot Pie (page 96) to the beloved Sweet and Sour Chicken (page 87), these dishes will have you passing up on takeout to whip up dinner at home!

BACON CHICKEN CAESAR CASSEROLE

MAKES: 5 servings

1 SERVING: 434 Calories, 31 g Fat, 6 g Carbs, 34 g Protein

||||||||||||||||||||||||||||||||||||||||||||||||||

6 oz (170 g) cream cheese, softened

½ cup (120 ml) chicken broth

⅓ cup (80 ml) sour cream

¼ cup (60 ml) mayo

½ tbsp (5 g) dried onion

2 tsp (5 g) garlic powder

1 lb (454 g) chicken breast, cooked and cubed

10 oz (300 g) fresh spinach

12 oz (340 g) broccoli florets (fresh or frozen)

¾ cup (75 g) Parmesan cheese, grated

4 strips thick-cut bacon, cooked and chopped, divided

½ cup (60 g) mozzarella cheese, shredded

The true MVP in the chicken dinner category goes to this hotshot. Quick, delicious and so full of greens, you can't help but lick the plate!

Preheat the oven to 350°F (176°C).

In a large bowl, combine the cream cheese, broth, sour cream, mayo, onion and garlic powder and mix thoroughly. Add the chicken, spinach, broccoli, Parmesan cheese and half of the bacon and mix well. Put the mixture in a 9 x 9–inch (23 x 23–cm) oven-safe dish and sprinkle with the remaining bacon and the mozzarella cheese.

Bake until hot and bubbling, about 30 minutes.

KASSEY'S KETO KASSEROLE

MAKES: 6 servings

1 SERVING: 437 Calories, 30 g Fat, 7 g Carbs, 28 g Protein

||||||||||||||||||||||||||||||||||||||||||||||||||

1 head of cauliflower, cut into bite-sized florets

1 head of broccoli, cut into bite-sized florets

1 cup (240 ml) heavy cream

5 tbsp (73 g) cream cheese

3 cloves garlic, minced

1 tsp onion powder

1 tsp salt

2 tsp (5 g) ground mustard

½ tsp black pepper

2 cups (226 g) Cheddar cheese, divided

8 strips thick-cut bacon

1½ lbs (681 g) chicken thighs

Casseroles are the backbone of weeknight dinners. They provide a tasty and nutritious meal for ourselves and our families. Kassey's Keto Kasserole is a mix of all your favorite Keto ingredients rolled into one creamy, cheesy, vegetable-filled casserole!

Preheat the oven to 350°F (176°C).

Steam the cauliflower and broccoli florets for 10 minutes. Set aside.

In a saucepan set over medium heat, add the heavy cream, cream cheese, garlic, onion powder, salt, ground mustard and black pepper. Slowly whisk for 3 minutes. Add 1½ cups (170 g) of the Cheddar cheese and whisk for 5 minutes. Set aside.

In a separate pan, fry the bacon and slice into small pieces. Reserve 2 tablespoons (30 ml) of the bacon fat and add to the cream sauce. Using the same pan, cook the chicken thighs until cooked through and no longer pink, 8 to 10 minutes. Dice the chicken into bite-sized pieces.

In a 9 x 13–inch (23 x 33–cm) casserole dish, combine the steamed vegetables, cream sauce, bacon and chicken. Mix well and top with the remaining ½ cup (56 g) of Cheddar cheese. Bake until the cheese has melted, about 20 minutes.

SWEET AND SOUR CHICKEN

MAKES: 5 servings

1 SERVING: 232 Calories, 7 g Fat,
3 g Carbs, 32 g Protein

||||||||||||||||||||||||||||||||||||||||||||||

CHICKEN

1½ lbs (681 g) chicken breast, diced

1 tsp salt

1 tsp garlic powder

Black pepper, to taste

1 tbsp (15 ml) olive oil

SAUCE

½ cup (60 g) erythritol (if you prefer less sweet, cut in half)

½ cup (120 ml) white vinegar

4 tbsp (60 ml) soy sauce

2 tsp (5 g) garlic powder

½ tsp onion powder

½ tsp chili powder

1 tsp sesame seed oil

¼ cup (60 ml) sugar-free or reduced-sugar ketchup

¼ tsp xanthan gum

Sweet and sour chicken is one of my all-time favorite dishes to get at a Chinese restaurant. And while this recipe is MAJORLY lacking in carbs and sugar, the flavor is spot on!

To prepare the chicken, season with the salt, garlic powder and black pepper. In a medium-sized skillet set over medium-high heat, add the olive oil and cook the chicken until it is cooked through and no longer pink, 8 to 9 minutes, stirring occasionally.

To make the sauce, in a large saucepan, simmer the erythritol, vinegar, soy sauce, garlic powder, onion powder, chili powder, sesame seed oil and ketchup. Once the mixture reaches a simmer, add the xanthan gum and stir until well mixed. Add the chicken to the sauce and stir well.

||||||||||||||||||||||||||||||||||||||||||||||||||||||||||||||||||||||||||||||||||||||||

TIP: If you'd like more veggies, add steamed broccoli florets into the sauce with the chicken.

MOUTHWATERING ITALIAN CHICKEN

MAKES: 4 servings

1 SERVING: 266 Calories, 16 g Fat, 3 g Carbs, 28 g Protein

||||||||||||||||||||||||||||||||||||||||||||||||

1 tbsp (15 ml) olive oil

1¼ lbs (567 g) chicken breast, quartered lengthwise

½ tsp salt

¼ tsp black pepper

3 cloves garlic, minced

1 tsp thyme

1½ tsp (4 g) red pepper flakes

¾ cup (180 ml) chicken broth

½ cup (120 ml) heavy cream

½ cup (100 g) cherry tomatoes, chopped

¼ cup (25 g) Parmesan cheese, freshly grated

¼ cup (12 g) fresh basil, roughly chopped

The name does not do this dish justice. In under 30 minutes, you will be fighting your family for the last serving of this anything-but-average chicken dinner!

Preheat the oven to 375°F (190°C).

In a large, oven-safe skillet, heat the olive oil over medium-high heat. While the olive oil is heating, quickly season the chicken with the salt and black pepper. Add the chicken to the skillet and sear until golden, about 2 to 3 minutes per side. Transfer to a plate and set aside.

Reduce the heat to medium and cook the garlic for 1 minute. Stir in the thyme, red pepper flakes, broth and heavy cream and cook for 5 minutes, stirring often. Stir in the tomatoes and Parmesan cheese. Return the chicken to the skillet and spoon the sauce all over. Transfer the skillet to the oven and bake until the chicken is cooked through, about 15 minutes. Garnish with the basil.

STICKY BOURBON CHICKEN

MAKES: 5 servings

1 SERVING: 285 Calories, 14 g Fat, 5 g Carbs, 31 g Protein

||||||||||||||||||||||||||||||||||||||||||||||||

1¼ lbs (567 g) boneless, skinless chicken breast, cut into 1-inch (2.5-cm) pieces, divided

3 tbsp (22 g) coconut flour

½ tsp salt

¼ tsp black pepper

4 tbsp (60 ml) olive oil, divided

2 cloves garlic, minced

1 cup (240 ml) water

¼ cup (60 ml) bourbon, or 2 tsp (10 ml) bourbon extract plus ¼ cup (60 ml) chicken broth

¾ cup (180 ml) chicken broth

⅔ cup (160 ml) soy sauce

2 tbsp (30 ml) sugar-free maple or pancake syrup

⅓ cup (80 ml) reduced-sugar ketchup

2 tbsp (30 ml) white vinegar

1 cup (115 g) brown sugar replacement (I recommend Swerve) or erythritol

½ tsp onion powder

½ tsp ground ginger

½ tsp crushed red pepper flakes

½ tsp xanthan gum

A comfort meal like no other, this Sticky Bourbon Chicken masterfully blends both sweet and savory flavors.

In a large bowl, toss the chicken with the coconut flour, salt and black pepper. In a nonstick skillet set over medium-high heat, add 2 tablespoons (30 ml) of the olive oil and let it heat for 45 seconds to 1 minute. Add half of the chicken and cook for 3 minutes without stirring, then turn the pieces and cook for an additional 3 minutes. Remove the chicken from the skillet and set aside. Repeat with the remaining olive oil and chicken.

Add the garlic to the skillet and cook until fragrant, about 20 seconds. Add the water, bourbon, broth, soy sauce, maple syrup, ketchup, vinegar, sugar replacement, onion powder, ginger and red pepper flakes. Bring the mixture to a boil and add the xanthan gum and whisk well. Reduce to a simmer, add the chicken to the sauce and cook for 10 to 15 minutes.

FIESTA CASSEROLE

MAKES: 5 servings

1 SERVING: 428 Calories, 30 g Fat, 7 g Carbs, 30 g Protein

||||||||||||||||||||||||||||||||||||||||||

CHICKEN

1 lb (454 g) chicken breast

1 cup (240 ml) sour cream

3 tbsp (45 g) taco seasoning (page 24)

18 oz (510 g) cauliflower rice, steamed, strained and squeezed of excess water

1 cup (113 g) Cheddar cheese, divided

SALSA

1 cup (200 g) Roma tomatoes, diced

¼ cup (40 g) red onion, diced

1 jalapeño pepper, diced

2 cloves garlic, minced

2 tbsp (7 g) cilantro

3 tbsp (45 ml) lime juice

¼ cup (60 ml) olive oil

½ tsp salt

¼ tsp black pepper

OPTIONAL GARNISHES

Sliced avocado

Chopped cilantro

Lime wedges

Even picky eaters will love this casserole! From the seasoning to the salsa, it's a fiesta in your mouth. Not to mention a great way to get in all your veggies. Add a scoop of guacamole or sour cream for a little more fat.

To cook the chicken, bring a large pot of water to a boil, add the chicken and boil for 12 minutes. Once cooked, use a mixer or two forks to shred the chicken.

To prepare the salsa, combine the tomatoes, red onion, jalapeño, garlic, cilantro, lime juice, olive oil, salt and black pepper. Mix well and set aside.

Preheat the oven to 350°F (176°C). Prepare a 9 x 13–inch (23 x 33–cm) baking dish with cooking spray and set aside.

In a large mixing bowl, combine the sour cream, taco seasoning and prepared salsa. Add the cauliflower rice and stir to combine. Add the chicken and half of the cheese. Stir to combine. Pour the mixture into the baking dish and sprinkle with the remaining cheese. Cover with aluminum foil and cook until the cheese is bubbling, about 20 minutes. If desired, garnish the casserole with sliced avocado, chopped cilantro and lime wedges.

||||||||||||||||||||||||||||||||||||||||||||||||||||||||||||||||||||||||

TIP: The optional garnishes are not included in the calculation of the macros. If you choose to use them, make sure to adjust the macros accordingly.

CRISPY CHICKEN TENDERS WITH CREAMY SPINACH

MAKES: 4 servings

1 SERVING: 476 Calories, 38 g Fat, 4 g Carbs, 30 g Protein

||||||||||||||||||||||||||||||||||||||||||||||||||

CHICKEN

1¼ lbs (567 g) boneless, skinless chicken breast, cut into chicken tender-sized pieces

¼ cup plus 2 tbsp (90 ml) extra-virgin olive oil, divided

¼ cup (60 ml) sour cream

¼ cup (60 ml) almond milk

1 tbsp (4 g) Italian seasoning

¼ cup (15 g) fresh parsley, chopped

4 cloves garlic, minced

Zest of 1 lemon

2 tbsp (30 ml) lemon juice

½ tsp salt

¼ tsp black pepper

SPINACH

3 tbsp (45 g) butter

½ tsp garlic powder

¼ tsp onion powder

10 oz (300 g) spinach, chopped

½ cup (120 ml) heavy cream

3 oz (90 g) cream cheese

¼ tsp salt

¼ tsp black pepper

1 tsp Italian seasoning

These chicken tenders are a step up from the drive-thru chicken nuggets of your childhood! They're crispy, flavorful and perfectly paired with the most amazing side dish—creamy spinach!

Place the chicken in a large zip-top bag. In a medium bowl, whisk ¼ cup (60 ml) of the olive oil, sour cream, almond milk, Italian seasoning, parsley, garlic, lemon zest, lemon juice, salt and black pepper. Pour the mixture over the chicken, seal the bag and shake to evenly coat with the marinade. Refrigerate for at least an hour, or up to 2 days.

Place a nonstick pan over medium-high heat, heat the remaining 2 tablespoons (30 ml) of the olive oil and cook the chicken until it is no longer pink in the middle, 6 to 8 minutes.

For the spinach, heat the butter in a large sauté pan or wok over medium heat. Add the garlic powder, onion powder and spinach, and sauté for 2 to 4 minutes, until wilted. If the pan is too full to stir at first, cover it for a minute or two to allow the spinach at the bottom to wilt, then you can start to stir in a folding motion. Once wilted, add the heavy cream, cream cheese, salt, black pepper and Italian seasoning. Stir constantly until the cream cheese melts, then cook for 3 to 4 minutes until thickened.

Serve the chicken tenders alongside the creamy spinach.

||||||||||||||||||||||||||||||||||||||||||||||||||||||||||||||||||||||

TIPS: To cook the chicken on an outdoor grill, heat the grill until hot and grill for 3 to 4 minutes on each side, until the chicken is no longer pink in the middle. Prepare the spinach as instructed above.

To cook the chicken in an Instant Pot, add ¼ cup (60 ml) of water to the bottom of the pot, wad up six balls of aluminum foil and place in the bottom of the cooker, and place the chicken directly on top of the foil. Cook on high pressure for 5 minutes and let it naturally release for 8 minutes. Prepare the spinach as instructed above.

CHICKEN POT PIE

MAKES: 6 servings

1 SERVING: 664 Calories, 53 g Fat, 6 g Carbs, 34 g Protein

|||||||||||||||||||||||||||||||||||||||||||||||||||

5 tbsp (75 g) butter, divided

¼ cup (60 ml) chicken broth

½ cup (120 ml) heavy whipping cream

½ tsp xanthan gum

3 bay leaves

1¾ tsp (2 g) thyme, divided

½ tsp paprika

¼ tsp cayenne

½ tsp salt, divided

¼ tsp black pepper

1½ cups (174 g) radishes, quartered

1 cup (150 g) green beans, chopped

¾ cup (78 g) celery, chopped

½ lb (227 g) chicken, cooked and shredded

2 tsp (3 g) parsley

2 cups (224 g) mozzarella cheese, shredded

4 oz (120 g) cream cheese

2 eggs, divided

2½ cups (260 g) almond flour

2 tsp (9 g) baking powder

1 tsp apple cider vinegar

¼ tsp rosemary

This classic homemade Keto-fied Chicken Pot Pie is the ultimate comfort food. A pan full of crisp, delicious veggies in a creamy seasoned sauce, topped with a thick and crispy crust, this is a recipe for perfection! Now I dare you not to go back for an extra bite!

To make the sauce, melt 3 tablespoons (45 g) of the butter in a saucepan over medium heat. Add in the broth, cream and xanthan gum, and mix until smooth and the mixture starts to bubble. Lower the heat to a gentle simmer and add the bay leaves, ½ teaspoon thyme, paprika, cayenne, ¼ teaspoon salt and black pepper. Continue to cook, whisking often, for about 3 to 4 minutes, or until the sauce has thickened. Remove the bay leaves and set the sauce aside.

Preheat the oven to 425°F (218°C).

Prepare the filling by melting the remaining 2 tablespoons (30 g) of butter in a large pan. Toss in the radishes, green beans and celery, and sauté for 2 to 3 minutes. Add in the chicken, 1 teaspoon of thyme and parsley. Remove from the heat and set aside.

Prepare the crust by melting the mozzarella and cream cheese in the microwave for 1 minute. Stir with a nonstick spoon and melt for an additional minute until smooth. Add 1 egg and stir to combine. Add the almond flour, baking powder and apple cider vinegar, and knead the dough well with damp hands. Season the crust with the remaining ¼ teaspoon salt, rosemary and the remaining ¼ teaspoon of thyme.

In a 9 x 9–inch (23 x 23–cm) square baking dish, add the chicken and vegetable mixture and drizzle with the sauce. Mix with a spatula to evenly coat. Divide the crust into fourths and flatten each piece between your hands, then place on top of the filling. Repeat until the top is fully covered. Whisk the remaining egg and brush over the top of the crust.

Bake for 25 to 30 minutes, until the crust is golden.

|||||||||||||||||||||||||||||||||||||||||||||||||||||||||||||||||||||||||||||

TIP: You can use shredded rotisserie chicken to make it easier.

SLOW COOKER CURRY CHICKEN

MAKES: 5 servings

1 SERVING: 207 Calories, 6 g Fat, 5 g Carbs, 31 g Protein

||||||||||||||||||||||||||||||||||||||||||

10 oz (300 ml) unsweetened canned coconut milk

8 oz (250 ml) chicken stock

3 tbsp (45 ml) lime juice

4 tbsp (6 g) basil leaves

1 tsp salt, plus more to taste

¾ tsp black pepper, plus more to taste

2 tbsp (12 g) yellow curry powder

1 tsp chili powder

½ cup (80 g) red onion, chopped

6 cloves garlic, minced

2 jalapeños, finely chopped

1½ lbs (681 g) chicken breast

1 tbsp (5 g) ground ginger

1½ tsp (7 g) xanthan gum, plus more as needed

½ cup (15 g) fresh cilantro, chopped

Finally, a dish you can just throw in the slow cooker without breaking a sweat! A traditional curry packed with flavor and melt-in-your-mouth, oh-so-tender chicken! This is a weeknight lineup winner.

To the slow cooker, add the coconut milk, chicken stock, lime juice, basil, salt, black pepper, curry powder and chili powder. Stir to combine. Add the onion, garlic and jalapeños. Stir. Add the chicken breast and stir again.

Cook until the chicken is fork tender and the sauce is fragrant, 4 to 5 hours on high or 6 to 8 hours on low.

Remove the chicken and transfer it to a plate or cutting board and allow it to rest for 5 to 7 minutes. Add the ginger to the slow cooker, stir, then add the xanthan gum and whisk until smooth. Add up to one more teaspoon of xanthan gum for a thicker sauce, a quarter teaspoon at a time. Shred the chicken and return it to the pot, cover and cook for an additional 10 minutes. Season with salt and black pepper, to taste, and stir in the cilantro.

||||||||||||||||||||||||||||||||||||||||||||||||||||||||||||||||||||||||||||||||

TIP: This can be made on the stovetop if you don't have a slow cooker or are short on time. Use already cooked chicken—either boiled or rotisserie. Combine all the ingredients, except the chicken and cilantro, in a large saucepan and cook on medium heat, stirring occasionally for 5 minutes. Once cooked, add in the shredded chicken and sprinkle with cilantro.

GRILLED MARGHERITA CHICKEN

MAKES: 4 servings

1 SERVING: 461 Calories, 35 g Fat, 3 g Carbs, 36 g Protein

||||||||||||||||||||||||||||||||||||||||||||||

PESTO

1 cup (24 g) fresh basil

2 cloves garlic, minced

2 tbsp (18 g) pine nuts

⅓ cup (33 g) Parmesan cheese, grated

½ tsp salt

½ tsp black pepper

¼ cup (60 ml) extra-virgin olive oil

CHICKEN

1 lb (454 g) boneless chicken breast, sliced in half lengthwise to make thin cutlets

Salt and black pepper, to taste

2 tbsp (30 ml) extra-virgin olive oil

2 tsp (5 g) garlic powder

1 tsp Italian seasoning

4 oz (120 g) mozzarella cheese, sliced

¼ cup (50 g) cherry tomatoes, halved

1 tbsp (15 ml) lemon juice

¼ cup (6 g) fresh basil, roughly chopped

A fresh margherita pizza is an Italian favorite. But how about combining all the things we love about a margherita pizza—the fresh mozzarella cheese, juicy tomatoes and fresh basil drizzled with olive oil—and adding them to simple, healthy, grilled chicken? *Mangia!*

Make the pesto in a blender. Add the basil, garlic, pine nuts, Parmesan cheese, salt and black pepper and blend for 30 to 45 seconds. Slowly drizzle in the olive oil and blend until well combined.

To prepare the chicken, in a large bowl toss the cutlets with the salt, black pepper, olive oil, garlic powder and Italian seasoning. Grill the chicken over medium-high heat for 6 to 8 minutes on each side, or until cooked through. Top each piece with a slice of mozzarella cheese and cook for another minute, or until melted.

Toss the tomatoes, lemon juice and basil together, and top each portion of the chicken with a quarter of the pesto and tomato mixture. Serve immediately.

CRANBERRY BAKED BRIE CHICKEN

MAKES: 6 servings

1 (6.1-OZ [170-G]) SERVING:
379 Calories, 29 g Fat, 6 g Carbs,
31 g Protein

IIIIIIIIIIIIIIIIIIIIIIIIIIIIIIIIIIIIIIIIIIII

CHICKEN AND FILLING

1½ lbs (681 g) boneless, skinless
chicken breasts

8 oz (225 g) cream cheese, softened

6 oz (170 g) spinach, chopped small

1 tsp garlic powder

¼ cup (32 g) pecans, chopped

¼ tsp ground black pepper

¼ tsp ground cloves

¼ tsp nutmeg

1 tsp salt

4 oz (120 g) brie cheese, chopped

2 tbsp (30 g) butter, melted

CRANBERRY SAUCE

6 oz (170 g) fresh cranberries

½ cup (120 ml) water

½ cup (60 g) erythritol

1 tbsp (15 ml) whiskey or bourbon,
or 1 tsp bourbon extract, optional

1 tbsp (15 ml) vanilla extract

While a festive dinner to be sure, this savory chicken stuffed with brie and topped with a slightly sweet and tart homemade cranberry sauce will be the star of the meal—whether it's July or November.

Preheat the oven to 375°F (190°C). Trim the chicken of any visible fat and membranes. Butterfly the chicken by cutting into the middle—being careful not to cut all the way through—so it opens like a book.

To prepare the filling, in a medium bowl, combine the cream cheese, spinach, garlic powder, pecans, black pepper, cloves, nutmeg and salt, and mix well. Divide the prepared filling and brie evenly and spoon into the butterflied chicken. Close the breasts and place in a 9 x 9–inch (23 x 23–cm) casserole dish. Drizzle the melted butter over the chicken.

Bake until the brie is melted, about 45 minutes.

To make the cranberry sauce, place the cranberries in a large pan with the water and erythritol. Bring to a boil over medium-high heat. Reduce to a simmer and add in the whiskey, if using, and vanilla. Simmer for 15 to 20 minutes, or until a thick consistency is reached. If you prefer a thicker consistency, boil longer, and if you prefer a thinner consistency, boil for less time. Set aside.

Divide the chicken into six portions and top each portion with 2 table-spoons (30 ml) of the cranberry sauce.

CHICKEN DIVAN CASSEROLE

MAKES: 6 servings

1 SERVING: 425 Calories, 32 g Fat, 4 g Carbs, 24 g Protein

||||||||||||||||||||||||||||||||||||||||||||

1 lb (454 g) chicken breasts

3 cups (300 g) cauliflower rice, steamed

3 tbsp (45 g) butter

½ tbsp (4 g) garlic powder

1 tsp garlic salt

½ tsp salt, plus more to taste

½ tsp parsley

½ tsp ground mustard

1 tsp black pepper

1 cup (240 ml) chicken broth

½ cup (120 ml) heavy cream

1 tsp lemon juice

½ cup (120 ml) mayo

3 cups (216 g) broccoli, chopped and steamed

1½ cups (170 g) Cheddar cheese, shredded

This classic chicken dish is brought back from my childhood and Keto-fied. This creamy "rice" dish is filled with chicken and broccoli and is tied together with a rich, cheesy sauce. It is also the perfect meal prep recipe, as it gets better each day! If you need more protein or fat for the day, add a sprinkle of bacon over the top.

Place the chicken breasts in a pot filled halfway with water. Bring to a boil over high heat and allow the chicken to cook for 15 to 20 minutes, or until cooked through. Remove from the pot and set aside to cool.

Preheat the oven to 350°F (176°C).

In a large pan or Dutch oven, add the cauliflower rice, butter, garlic powder, garlic salt, salt, parsley, ground mustard, black pepper and broth. Cover and cook for 5 minutes.

Add the cream and lemon juice to the pan and let simmer uncovered on low for 10 minutes. Mix a few times throughout so it doesn't burn on the bottom. Add the mayo, mix and turn the burner off.

Shred the chicken with a fork and place half of the chicken into the cauliflower cream mixture. Put the remaining chicken into the bottom of an 8 x 8–inch (20 x 20–cm) casserole dish and top with the broccoli, cream mixture and Cheddar cheese.

Cover with aluminum foil and cook for 20 minutes. Remove the foil and bake until bubbling, about 10 minutes.

GREEK "RICE" BOWL

MAKES: 4 servings

1 SERVING: 417 Calories, 29 g Fat, 6 g Carbs, 29 g Protein

||||||||||||||||||||||||||||||||||||||||||||||

GREEK DRESSING

¼ cup (60 ml) extra-virgin olive oil

¼ cup (60 ml) lemon juice

½ tbsp (7 ml) red wine vinegar

4 cloves garlic, minced

1½ tbsp (5 g) oregano

1 tsp salt

½ tsp black pepper

CHICKEN

1 lb (454 g) boneless, skinless chicken thighs (about 4 thighs)

1 tbsp (15 ml) extra-virgin olive oil

"RICE" BOWL

12 oz (340 g) cauliflower rice, steamed

½ cup (65 g) cucumber, chopped

¼ cup (40 g) red onion, chopped

½ cup (100 g) Roma tomatoes, chopped

15 Kalamata olives, sliced

½ cup (75 g) feta cheese, crumbled

Greek food is always so flavorful and fresh—full of vegetables, olives, feta and just the perfect amount of tartness from a squeeze of lemon. This hearty "rice" bowl is no exception. The Mediterranean flavors transform a simple cauliflower rice bowl into a lunchtime culinary masterpiece in under 15 minutes!

To make the dressing, in a small mixing bowl, whisk the olive oil, lemon juice, vinegar, garlic, oregano, salt and black pepper. Reserve about ¼ cup (60 ml) of the dressing for finishing.

To prepare the chicken, place it in a large, resealable plastic bag with the non-reserved dressing. Massage the dressing into the chicken and refrigerate for at least 2 hours, and up to overnight. After marinating, heat a large skillet over medium-high heat with the olive oil and cook the chicken for 4 to 5 minutes per side, or until golden and cooked through. Remove to a plate.

To assemble the bowls, divide the cauliflower rice evenly among individual serving dishes and top with the cucumber, red onion, tomatoes, olives, chicken and feta. Drizzle the reserved dressing evenly over the bowls.

CREAMY GARLIC CHICKEN

MAKES: 5 servings

1 SERVING: 324 Calories, 22 g Fat, 3 g Carbs, 29 g Protein

|||||||||||||||||||||||||||||||||||||||||||||||

3 tbsp (45 g) butter, divided

1¼ lbs (567 g) chicken breast, chopped into bite-sized pieces

½ tsp Italian seasoning

½ tsp salt, plus more to taste

¼ tsp black pepper, plus more to taste

½ cup (120 ml) chicken broth

1 tbsp (9 g) garlic, minced

1 tbsp (7 g) parsley

½ cup (120 ml) heavy cream

½ cup (120 ml) unsweetened almond milk

¼ tsp xanthan gum

½ cup (50 g) Parmesan cheese, freshly grated or shredded

This recipe features a creamy garlic sauce smothering tender bite-sized pieces of chicken. Serve it over mashed faux-tatoes or cauliflower rice to soak up all the delicious sauce.

In a large nonstick pan over medium-high heat, melt 1 tablespoon (15 g) of the butter. While the butter is melting, season the chicken pieces with the Italian seasoning, salt and black pepper. When the butter has melted, add the chicken to the pan and cook for 5 to 6 minutes on each side, or until golden brown and cooked through. Remove from the pan and set aside.

Melt the remaining 2 tablespoons (30 g) of the butter in the pan, add the broth and bring to a simmer. Cook for 3 to 4 minutes, or until the broth is reduced by about half. Add the garlic, parsley, cream, almond milk and xanthan gum, and simmer for 3 to 4 minutes.

Stir in the Parmesan cheese and continue to stir until the sauce has thickened. Season with salt and black pepper to taste. Add the chicken to the pan and cover with the sauce. Serve immediately.

||||||||||||||||||||||||||||||||||||||||||||||||||||||||||||||||||||||||||||||||||||||

TIPS: If you want to make this dairy-free, use coconut cream in place of the heavy cream, dairy-free butter and an additional ½ teaspoon of xanthan gum. Be sure to omit the Parmesan cheese.

If you have the macros, this tastes great with crumbled bacon on top!

Don't Go Bacon My Heart!
TELL ME, WHERE'S THE BEEF?

While I do love bacon, a good steak and a bunless burger, sometimes you want to venture out of your comfort zone. Keto doesn't need to be boring or repetitive. It can be flavorful and full of variety. The cheesy Mozzarella Meatball Casserole (page 112), the soul-feeding Stuffed Pepper Soup (page 126) and the super flavorful Legit Steak (page 142) all deliver a punch of flavor that could tempt even a vegetarian!

MOZZARELLA MEATBALL CASSEROLE

MAKES: 6 servings

1 SERVING (2 MEATBALLS): 438 Calories, 30 g Fat, 7 g Carbs, 32 g Protein

||||||||||||||||||||||||||||||||||||||||||||||||||

MARINARA SAUCE

1 (28-oz [785-g]) can no-sugar-added peeled tomatoes, with liquid

¼ cup (60 ml) extra-virgin olive oil

1 tbsp (15 ml) white vinegar

¼ tsp black pepper

1 tsp red pepper flakes

1 tsp onion powder

1 tsp garlic powder

1 tsp basil

1 tsp oregano

1 tsp parsley

1 tsp erythritol

1 tsp salt, plus more as needed

It doesn't get any easier than this recipe to make an authentic Italian meatball dinner. Even your picky eaters will be gobbling this one up! For those looking to go *Lady and the Tramp* style, serve over zoodles!

To make the marinara sauce, combine the tomatoes, olive oil, vinegar, black pepper, red pepper flakes, onion powder, garlic powder, basil, oregano, parsley, erythritol and salt in a large pot and simmer for 40 minutes. Use an immersion blender to blend until smooth. Set aside. The recipe will make excess sauce. You will only need 10 ounces (300 ml).

Preheat the oven to 400°F (204°C). Line an oven-safe skillet with aluminum foil and set aside.

(continued)

MEATBALLS

½ lb (227 g) ground pork

¾ lb (340 g) ground beef

6 cloves garlic, minced

12 oz (340 g) cauliflower rice, steamed

½ cup (52 g) almond flour

½ cup (50 g) Parmesan cheese, shredded

3 tbsp (12 g) fresh parsley, chopped

2 eggs

½ tsp salt

¼ tsp black pepper

½ cup (56 g) mozzarella cheese, shredded

1 tbsp (15 ml) olive oil

½ tsp Italian seasoning

To make the meatballs, in a large bowl, combine the ground meats, garlic, cauliflower rice, almond flour, Parmesan cheese, parsley, eggs, salt and black pepper. Mix with your hands until just combined. Be careful not to overmix. Form into meatballs. I like to weigh the meat and divide it into equal-sized balls. Each meatball should be approximately 3.3 ounces (90 g).

Coat the prepared skillet with cooking spray and bake the meatballs for 10 minutes. Remove from the oven and lower the temperature to 375°F (190°C). Place the meatballs on a plate and remove the foil from the skillet. Pour ½ cup (120 ml) of the marinara sauce in the bottom of the skillet, spreading evenly. Place the meatballs in a single layer over the marinara sauce and pour the remaining sauce over the meatballs. Sprinkle with the mozzarella cheese, drizzle with the olive oil and sprinkle with the Italian seasoning.

Cover the skillet with aluminum foil and bake for 20 minutes. Remove the foil and bake uncovered until the cheese is melted, about 20 minutes.

|||||||||||||||||||||||||||||||||||||||||||||||||||||||||||||||||||||||||||||||||||||||

TIPS: If you don't want to make your own sauce, you can use a store-bought one, such as Rao's, or a brand that has 4 grams net carbs per ½ cup (120 ml). If you can't find one, feel free to use pureed tomatoes mixed with ½ teaspoon of Italian seasoning.

To make this dairy-free, omit the mozzarella and Parmesan cheese and add ½ cup (30 g) of crushed pork rinds.

MAPLE-BOURBON MEATBALLS

MAKES: 35 meatballs

1 SERVING (1 MEATBALL): 163 Calories, 14 g Fat, 1 g Carbs, 10 g Protein

||||||||||||||||||||||||||||||||||||||||||||||||||

BBQ SAUCE

2 tbsp (30 g) butter

¼ cup (40 g) onions, diced

1 tsp maple extract

½ tsp bourbon extract or 1 tbsp (15 ml) bourbon

¼ cup (60 ml) soy sauce

¼ cup (60 ml) white vinegar

½ tsp chili paste (I recommend Sambal Oelek)

1 tbsp (15 ml) Dijon mustard

2 tbsp (30 ml) fresh lemon juice

¾ cup (180 ml) reduced-sugar ketchup

5 tbsp (40 g) brown sugar replacement (I recommend Swerve)

1 tsp garlic powder

½ tsp onion powder

½ tsp chili powder

½ tsp black pepper

These sweet and tangy meatballs are always a hit as an appetizer or meal. They are amazing served over mashed faux-tatoes to soak up all the delicious sauce.

To prepare the BBQ sauce, in a medium saucepan over medium-high heat, melt the butter and sauté the onions until translucent and softened, 2 to 3 minutes. Add the maple extract, bourbon extract, soy sauce, vinegar, chili paste, mustard, lemon juice, ketchup, sugar replacement, garlic powder, onion powder, chili powder and black pepper. Bring the mixture to a boil then turn to low and cook the sauce for 20 to 35 minutes, stirring occasionally until thickened.

Preheat the oven to 400°F (204°C). Line a baking sheet with aluminum foil and set aside.

(continued)

MEATBALLS

1 lb (454 g) thick-cut bacon

1½ lbs (681 g) ground pork

1½ lbs (681 g) ground beef

1 egg

½ cup (50 g) Parmesan cheese, shredded

¼ cup (26 g) ground flaxseed

1 tsp salt

1 tsp black pepper

2 tsp (5 g) garlic powder

MAPLE-BOURBON SAUCE

1 cup (125 g) erythritol

3 tbsp (45 g) chili paste

½ cup (120 ml) bourbon or 2 tsp (10 ml) bourbon extract

1 cup (240 ml) BBQ sauce (prepared on page 115)

5 tbsp (75 ml) sugar-free pancake syrup

½ cup (120 ml) water

To make the meatballs, place the bacon into a food processor and blend until a paste is formed. Add the paste to a bowl with the pork and beef and mix in the egg, Parmesan cheese, flaxseed, salt, black pepper and garlic powder. Thoroughly mix with your hands and form into meatballs. Place on the prepared baking sheet and bake for 35 to 40 minutes, or until browned.

To prepare the maple-bourbon sauce, in a saucepan set over medium heat, combine the erythritol, chili paste, bourbon, prepared BBQ sauce, syrup and water, stirring frequently until the edges start to bubble.

Add the meatballs and maple-bourbon sauce to a slow cooker set to low. Cook for 2 to 3 hours. Alternatively, you can use a stock pot or Dutch oven on the stovetop. Adjust the cooking time to 20 minutes.

LOADED CHUNKY CHILI

MAKES: 12 servings

1 SERVING: 210 Calories, 11 g Fat, 4 g Carbs, 20 g Protein

||||||||||||||||||||||||||||||||||||||||||||||||||

1¾ lbs (794 g) 80/20 ground beef

8 strips bacon

1 large green bell pepper, chopped

1 habanero pepper, finely chopped (add more or less to your taste)

1 jalapeño, finely chopped

¼ cup (40 g) yellow onion, chopped

1 (20-oz [560-g]) can diced tomatoes, with liquid

12 oz (340 g) pureed tomatoes

½ cup (120 ml) chicken broth

1 tbsp (7 g) paprika

2 tbsp (10 g) ground cumin

3 cloves garlic, minced

2 tbsp (14 g) chipotle powder

1 tbsp (7 g) oregano

½ tsp cayenne pepper

1 tsp cinnamon

Salt and black pepper, to taste

Say it loud enough for those in the back! This chili is A.M.A.Z.I.N.G. I have won two chili cookoff contests with this recipe! A perfect balance of spice and flavor, this hearty chili pairs well with my "Hold the Corn" Corn Bread (page 121). For those that need a little more fat, feel free to top with a dollop of sour cream and/or sliced avocado.

Brown the beef in a large skillet, reserving half of the rendered fat. In the same skillet, fry the bacon. Remove from the pan and chop. Drain the fat from the pan and add the bell pepper, habanero, jalapeño and yellow onion, cooking for 2 minutes.

In the bowl of the slow cooker, add the beef and rendered fat, diced and pureed tomatoes, bacon, cooked peppers and onion, broth, paprika, cumin, garlic, chipotle powder, oregano, cayenne and cinnamon.

Cook on low for 5 hours or on high for 3 hours. Season with salt and black pepper.

||||||||||||||||||||||||||||||||||||||||||||||||||||||||||||||||||||||

TIPS: This can be cooked in a stock pot or Dutch oven. Adjust the cooking time to 30 minutes.

The chili freezes very well!

"HOLD THE CORN" CORN BREAD

MAKES: 10 servings

1 SERVING: 198 Calories, 17 g Fat, 1 g Carbs, 9 g Protein

||||||||||||||||||||||||||||||||||||||||||||||||

2 cups (226 g) Cheddar cheese, shredded

2 cups (208 g) almond flour

3 tbsp (21 g) erythritol

2 tsp (9 g) baking powder

½ tsp garlic powder

½ tsp salt

3 large eggs

½ cup (120 ml) sour cream

¼ cup (60 g) butter, melted

Moist and slightly sweet, this "Hold the Corn" Corn Bread has the consistency you would expect from this Southern staple.

Preheat the oven to 350°F (176°C). Grease a 9 x 13–inch (23 x 33–cm) glass baking dish and set aside.

In a large bowl, combine the cheese, almond flour, erythritol, baking powder, garlic powder and salt. In a separate bowl, whisk together the eggs, sour cream and butter. Add the wet ingredients to the dry, stirring until well combined.

Pour the batter into the baking dish, spreading evenly, and bake for 20 to 25 minutes, or until the edges begin to brown. Let cool for a few minutes before cutting.

||||||||||||||||||||||||||||||||||||||||||||||||||||||||||||||||||||||||||||||||||||||||||||||

TIP: You can enhance the flavor by adding 5 drops of corn bread extract to the batter. I have made it with and without—it's good either way!

BEEF BOURGUIGNON

MAKES: 6 servings

1 SERVING: 329 Calories, 17 g Fat, 5 g Carbs, 30 g Protein

IIIIIIIIIIIIIIIIIIIIIIIIIIIIIIIIIIIIIIIIIIIIIIIII

8 strips bacon, roughly chopped

1½ lbs (681 g) beef brisket or stewing beef, cut into 2-inch (5-cm) chunks and patted dry

½ cup (80 g) white onion, diced

3 cloves garlic, minced

½ tsp coarse salt, plus more as needed

¼ tsp freshly ground black pepper, plus more as needed

2 tbsp (15 g) coconut flour

1½ cups (360 ml) red wine (Pinot Noir or Chianti)

1 cup (240 ml) beef stock

2 tbsp (30 g) tomato paste

½ tsp thyme

2 tsp (3 g) parsley

1 bay leaf

2 tbsp (30 g) butter, salted

½ lb (227 g) fresh small white mushrooms, quartered

A French staple with flavors that will have your friends and family thinking Julia Child was in the kitchen, this will be the most flavorful stew you have EVER tasted!

In a large Dutch oven or pot set over medium heat, sauté the bacon until crisp and browned. Transfer the bacon to a large dish, reserving the rendered fat in the pot. Sear the beef in the same pot in batches for 3 to 4 minutes, or until all sides are browned. Remove to the same dish as the bacon. Add the onion and sauté until softened, about 3 minutes. Add the garlic and cook for 1 minute. Return the bacon and beef to the pot, season with the salt and black pepper and sprinkle with the coconut flour. Toss well and cook for 4 to 5 minutes, until browned. Add the wine and stock, stir, then add the tomato paste, thyme, parsley and bay leaf. Cover and bring to a boil, then reduce the heat to low and simmer for 1½ to 2 hours, stirring occasionally, until the meat is falling apart.

During the last 5 minutes of cooking, heat the butter in a medium-sized skillet set over medium heat and cook the mushrooms for 5 minutes, until browned. Season with salt and black pepper, if desired. Add the mushrooms to the stew and let simmer for 3 to 5 minutes, stirring occasionally.

SPEEDY MEATLOAF

MAKES: 8 servings

1 SERVING: 313 Calories, 20 g Fat, 6 g Carbs, 26 g Protein

||||||||||||||||||||||||||||||||||||||||||||||

MEATLOAF

½ cup (110 g) crushed tomatoes

½ cup (50 g) Parmesan cheese, grated

½ cup (52 g) almond flour

½ cup (120 ml) unsweetened almond milk

2 eggs

2 tbsp (15 g) parsley

2 tbsp (30 ml) soy sauce

¾ lb (340 g) ground beef

¾ lb (340 g) ground pork

¼ cup (40 g) red onion, diced

3 cloves garlic, minced

½ tsp salt

¼ tsp black pepper

SAUCE

½ cup (120 ml) reduced-sugar ketchup

2 tbsp (15 g) brown sugar replacement (I recommend Swerve), erythritol or monk fruit

1½ tsp (8 ml) white vinegar

½ tsp chili powder

Not your school lunch special, this moist meatloaf is full of flavor and topped with a tangy, sweet and oh-so-perfect sauce! And if you just so happen to have leftovers, it tastes even better the next day.

Preheat the oven to 375°F (190°C).

In a large bowl, using your hands, mix the tomatoes, Parmesan cheese, almond flour, almond milk, eggs, parsley, soy sauce, beef, pork, onion, garlic, salt and black pepper. Press into a 9 x 13–inch (23 x 33–cm) baking dish. Bake until the meatloaf is formed and you see the sides start to bubble, 20 minutes.

While the meatloaf is cooking, prepare the sauce. In a small bowl, whisk the ketchup, sugar replacement, vinegar and chili powder. Set aside.

Once the meatloaf is cooked, remove from the oven and brush the sauce over the top. Return to the oven and broil for 2 to 3 minutes.

||||||||||||||||||||||||||||||||||||||||||||||||||||||||||||||||||||||||||||

TIP: To make this dairy-free, substitute crushed pork rinds for the Parmesan cheese. Macros for this option: 312 Calories, 20 g Fat, 5 g Carbs, 27 g Protein.

STUFFED PEPPER SOUP

MAKES: 5 servings

1 SERVING: 291 Calories, 19 g Fat, 7 g Carbs, 18 g Protein

||||||||||||||||||||||||||||||||||||||||||||||||||

2 tbsp (30 ml) olive oil, divided

¾ lb (340 g) ground beef

¼ tsp salt, plus more to season

¼ tsp black pepper, plus more to season

½ cup (80 g) yellow onion, chopped

¾ cup (112 g) red bell pepper, chopped

¾ cup (112 g) green bell pepper, chopped

2 cloves garlic, minced

1 (8-oz [225-g]) can petite diced tomatoes, with liquid

1 (12-oz [340-g]) jar tomato sauce (I recommend Rao's or another low-carb option)

32 oz (1 L) beef broth

2½ tbsp (10 g) fresh parsley, chopped, plus more for optional garnish

½ tsp basil

¼ tsp oregano

12 oz (340 g) cauliflower rice, steamed

One of my all-time favorite Italian dishes was stuffed peppers. I loved the flavor, but they always left me wanting more and more. I decided to turn this beloved recipe into a soup, and not only is it one of my all-time favorite soups, but the delicious broth helps to make it more satiating!

In a large pot set over medium heat, warm 1 tablespoon (15 ml) of the olive oil. Once the oil is hot, add the beef, salt and black pepper and cook, stirring occasionally, until the meat is browned. Remove from the pot and set aside.

Add the remaining tablespoon (15 ml) of olive oil to the pot and add the onion and bell peppers, sauté for 3 minutes, then add the garlic and sauté for an additional 30 seconds. Pour in the diced tomatoes, tomato sauce, broth, parsley, basil, oregano, cauliflower rice and cooked beef. Season with salt and black pepper. Bring the mixture to a light boil, reduce the heat to low and simmer, covered, for 30 minutes. Stir occasionally. Garnish with fresh parsley, if desired.

||||||||||||||||||||||||||||||||||||||||||||||||||||||||||||||||||

TIPS: This soup freezes very well.

If you need more fat, add a little sour cream to the top.

If you like spicy food, add 2 tablespoons (14 g) of red pepper flakes.

BEEF AND BROCCOLI

MAKES: 5 servings

1 SERVING: 307 Calories, 19 g Fat, 3 g Carbs, 33 g Protein

||||||||||||||||||||||||||||||||||||||||||||

BEEF

1 tbsp (15 ml) olive oil

1½ lbs (681 g) flank or hanger steak, sliced no thicker than ¼ inch (6 mm)

6 cups (432 g) broccoli florets

½ cup (120 ml) beef stock

SAUCE

½ cup (120 ml) soy sauce

½ cup (60 g) brown sugar replacement (I recommend Swerve or Sukrin Gold) or plain erythritol

2 tbsp (30 ml) white vinegar

2 tbsp (30 ml) sesame oil

4 cloves garlic, minced

½ tsp chili paste

½ tsp onion powder

½ to 1 tsp xanthan gum

This is a favorite Chinese dish of mine with a Keto spin! Flank steak—seared and juicy—tossed in a sweet and savory garlic chili sauce. Broccoli is mixed in to make a deliciously well-balanced entrée. Having this recipe in your kitchen arsenal will keep you on track and stop you from ordering out.

To make the beef, heat the olive oil in a pan set over medium heat for a few minutes. Add the sliced beef and stir frequently until it browns, about 2 to 3 minutes. Be sure not to overcook. Transfer the beef to a plate and set aside. Add the broccoli and stock to the same pan and bring to a simmer. Cook, stirring occasionally, until the broccoli is tender, about 6 minutes.

While waiting for the broccoli to cook, make the sauce by combining the soy sauce, sugar replacement, vinegar, sesame oil, garlic, chili paste, onion powder and xanthan gum. Mix well.

Once the broccoli has cooked, add the beef and sauce to the pan, stir, and simmer for 5 minutes, until the sauce thickens. Serve over cooked cauliflower rice or sautéed veggies.

LOADED HALLOUMI FRIES

MAKES: 4 servings

1 SERVING: 459 Calories, 39 g Fat, 3 g Carbs, 24 g Protein

||||||||||||||||||||||||||||||||||||||||||||||||||

SAUCE

3 tbsp (45 ml) sugar-free ketchup

¼ cup (60 ml) mayo

½ tsp white vinegar

¼ tsp paprika

¼ tsp brown sugar replacement
(I recommend Swerve) or erythritol

Pinch of black pepper

Pinch of salt

HALLOUMI FRIES

½ cup (120 g) coconut oil

1½ lbs (681 g) halloumi cheese

½ tsp oregano

½ tsp garlic powder

½ tsp onion powder

¼ tsp paprika

¼ tsp cayenne pepper, optional
(omit if you do not like spicy)

TOPPING

8 strips bacon, cooked and chopped

1 tbsp (3 g) dried chives

Fries were honestly the only thing I missed until I developed this recipe. These Loaded Halloumi Fries will satisfy your french fry cravings, without the carbs, especially when dipped into a "special" sauce with sweet and tart notes.

Make the sauce by combining the ketchup, mayo, vinegar, paprika, sugar replacement, black pepper and salt. Set aside.

To prepare the halloumi, heat the coconut oil in a shallow pan over medium-high heat. While the oil is heating, slice the halloumi into "fries" about ½ inch (1.25 cm) thick. Be careful not to cut too thin. Sprinkle with the oregano, garlic powder, onion powder, paprika and cayenne pepper, if using. Fry in the coconut oil until the halloumi fries are golden brown, 4 to 5 minutes per side.

Top with the chopped bacon and chives.

|||||||||||||||||||||||||||||||||||||||||||||||||||||||||||||||||||||||||||||||||||||||||

TIP: You can make these in the air fryer. Cook at 390°F (200°C) for 8 to 10 minutes.

CAJUN PORK CHOPS

MAKES: 4 servings

1 SERVING (1 CHOP): 388 Calories, 21 g Fat, 3 g Carbs, 22 g Protein

||||||||||||||||||||||||||||||||||||||||||||||||||||||

4 (4-oz [120-g]) thick-cut pork chops

½ tsp salt, plus more as needed

½ tsp black pepper, plus more as needed

2 tbsp (30 g) butter

½ cup (40 g) mushrooms, sliced

1 tbsp (10 g) garlic powder

1 cup (240 ml) chicken broth

2 bay leaves

½ cup (120 ml) sour cream

1 oz (30 g) cream cheese

½ tsp cayenne pepper

¼ tsp crushed red pepper

1 tsp paprika

½ tsp onion powder

½ tsp oregano

½ tsp thyme

This recipe features juicy, tender chops with a delicious, creamy sauce and a New Orleans kick of spice. This dinner will bring a little bit of the South to your plate.

Season the chops with the salt and black pepper. Heat the butter in a large skillet over medium-high heat and cook the chops until browned, about 5 minutes per side. Remove the chops from the pan and set aside. Leave the fat in the skillet. Add the mushrooms to the skillet and sauté until softened, about 5 minutes, then add the garlic powder and a pinch of salt, and cook for about 30 seconds.

Add the broth to deglaze the pan and scrape all the browned bits loose, then turn it down to a simmer. Add the bay leaves and place the chops back in the sauce. Cover and simmer on low for 30 to 35 minutes, until the chops are cooked through. Remove the chops from the pan to a plate and loosely cover with foil.

Increase the heat to high and bring the pan juices to a boil for 8 minutes, or until the sauce has reduced by about half. Remove the bay leaves and turn the heat down to low. Add the sour cream, cream cheese, cayenne pepper, crushed red pepper, paprika, onion powder, oregano and thyme. Whisk until smooth and creamy, heating for 3 minutes. Be sure not to boil the sauce. Taste and adjust with salt and black pepper. Add the chops back to the pan and coat in the sauce, then heat for 1 to 2 minutes.

CREAMY TORTILLA SOUP

MAKES: 7 servings

1 SERVING: 333 Calories, 17 g Fat, 7 g Carbs, 32 g Protein

||||||||||||||||||||||||||||||||||||||||||||||||||

3½ cups (840 ml) chicken broth

1 lb (454 g) chicken breasts, cooked and shredded

½ lb (227 g) pork chops, thinly sliced and cut into quarter-sized pieces

⅓ cup (53 g) onion, chopped

½ tsp ground cumin

2 cloves garlic, minced

¼ to 1 tsp cayenne pepper, depending on spice level preference

1 tbsp (15 ml) olive oil

8 oz (225 g) diced tomatoes

6 oz (170 g) tomato puree

1 to 4 oz (30 to 120 g) canned diced green chiles

¼ cup (4 g) fresh cilantro, chopped

2 tsp oregano

12 oz (340 g) cabbage, shredded

8 oz (225 g) cream cheese

Full of flavor and just the right amount of spice, this hearty soup will have you licking your bowl clean!

In a slow cooker, add the broth, chicken, pork, onion, cumin, garlic, cayenne pepper, olive oil, diced tomatoes, tomato puree, chiles, cilantro, oregano and cabbage. Cook on low for 4 to 5 hours. Add the cream cheese and cook for an additional hour.

||||||||||||||||||||||||||||||||||||||||||||||||||

TIPS: You can also cook this on the stove in a stock pot on medium-low heat for 30 minutes.

You can increase the spiciness by using a habanero pepper instead of green chiles.

PIZZA POT PIE

MAKES: 6 servings

1 SERVING: 352 Calories, 27 g Fat, 7 g Carbs, 19 g Protein

IIIIIIIIIIIIIIIIIIIIIIIIIIIIIIIIIIIIIIIII

DOUGH

1 tbsp (15 g) butter for greasing the pan

1 cup (104 g) almond flour

3 tbsp (20 g) coconut flour

2 tsp (9 g) xanthan gum

1 (¼-oz [7-g]) packet instant yeast

1 tsp baking powder

¼ tsp salt

½ tsp garlic powder

2 tsp (4 g) Italian seasoning

2 tsp (10 ml) water

1 egg

FILLING

1 tbsp (15 g) butter

1 cup (74 g) broccoli, chopped

½ cup (75 g) green bell pepper, chopped

1 cup (68 g) white mushrooms, chopped

3 cloves garlic, minced

1 tsp oregano

¼ tsp salt

¼ tsp black pepper

5 strips bacon, cooked and crumbled

1 cup (240 ml) marinara sauce (page 112, see Tips)

1½ cups (168 g) mozzarella cheese, shredded

2 oz (57 g) sliced pepperoni, roughly chopped

Inspired by Chicago-style deep-dish pizzas, I had to take a stab at my own Keto version and, in all honesty, it doesn't disappoint. A light crispy crust, a warm cheesy center and a sauce with some bite, this recipe is the start of something beautiful! You have the freedom to switch up the filling and go more meat or veggie heavy. I chose veggie because I am the queen of greens! What will you fill yours with?

Preheat the oven to 400°F (204°C). Grease a 9-inch (23-cm) skillet or pie pan with the butter.

To make the dough, in a large bowl, whisk the almond flour, coconut flour, xanthan gum, yeast, baking powder, salt, garlic powder and Italian seasoning. In a small bowl, mix the water and egg, then combine with the dough mixture. Use damp hands to knead the dough into a ball. Press the dough into the prepared pan, making sure to push it up along the sides of the pan. Bake for 8 minutes, or until golden. Allow to cool.

While the dough is cooling, prepare the filling. Melt the butter in another skillet over medium-high heat. Add the broccoli, bell pepper and mushrooms and sauté for 5 minutes, tossing occasionally. Add the garlic, oregano, salt and black pepper and mix well. Add the veggie mixture, bacon and marinara sauce to the dough. Sprinkle with the cheese. Bake for 20 to 25 minutes. Top with the pepperoni and return to the oven until the cheese has melted, about 5 minutes.

IIIIIIIIIIIIIIIIIIIIIIIIIIIIIIIIIIIIIIIIIIIIIIIIIIIIIIIIIIIIIIIIIIIIIIIIIIIIIIIIIIIIIIIII

TIPS: You can always switch up the fillings and topping and adjust the macros.

Instead of making your own marinara, you can use a store-bought, low-carb version, such as Rao's.

BEEF VINDALOO

MAKES: 4 servings

1 SERVING: 246 Calories, 13 g Fat, 6 g Carbs, 26 g Protein

½ cup (80 g) onion, diced

5 cloves garlic, minced

2 tsp (4 g) ground ginger

1 tbsp (15 ml) olive oil

¼ cup (60 ml) white vinegar

1 cup (200 g) tomato, diced

1 tsp salt

1 tsp garam masala

1 tsp paprika

½ to 3 tsp (1 to 5 g) cayenne pepper (adjust to desired spice level)

½ tsp coriander

1 tsp ground cumin

½ tsp turmeric

¼ cup (60 ml) beef broth

1 lb (454 g) stewing beef

I am a sucker for good Indian food. The aromas are entrancing, and the sauces are always to die for. This Beef Vindaloo is just that. Full of flavor, it will have your kitchen smelling amazing—with very little effort on your part. And for those that enjoy that traditional Indian heat, kick up the spiciness by mixing in ½ tablespoon (8 g) of chili paste.

In a blender or food processor, combine the onion, garlic, ginger, olive oil, vinegar, tomato, salt, garam masala, paprika, cayenne pepper, coriander, cumin, turmeric and broth. Once blended, pour into a zip-top bag with the beef. Allow to marinate for 20 minutes, or up to overnight.

In a Dutch oven or a very large skillet set over medium-high heat, cook the beef with the marinade, covered, until fork tender, 30 to 35 minutes.

TIP: This can be made in an Instant Pot®. Cook the marinade and beef on high pressure for 10 minutes, then allow to naturally release for 10 minutes.

KETO SHEPHERD'S PIE

MAKES: 5 servings

1 SERVING: 475 Calories, 36 g Fat, 5 g Carbs, 28 g Protein

||||||||||||||||||||||||||||||||||||||||||||||

1½ lbs (681 g) 80/20 ground beef

¼ cup (40 g) yellow onion, chopped

2 cloves garlic, minced

1 tsp soy sauce

½ cup (120 ml) beef broth

20 oz (560 g) cauliflower florets or cauliflower rice, steamed and well drained

½ cup (57 g) Cheddar cheese, shredded, divided

3 tbsp (45 ml) sour cream

2 tbsp (30 g) butter, melted

½ tsp salt

We have covered so many cultural dishes so far, and I would be thoughtless if I left out a good Irish recipe. So jig right over to your stove for this quick, kid-pleasing dinner. The smooth, creamy mashed faux-tatoes take the place of traditional potatoes—but don't worry, they are good enough to fool those with an anti-cauliflower agenda. This is a great simple, satisfying weeknight meal for when you are short on time.

Preheat the oven to broil.

Cook the beef, onion and garlic in a large frying pan over medium-high heat for 5 to 7 minutes, stirring frequently, until the beef is thoroughly cooked. Drain. Stir in the soy sauce and broth and simmer, covered, for 2 minutes. Stir occasionally.

In a blender or food processor, combine the cauliflower, ¼ cup (28 g) of the cheese, sour cream, butter and salt and process until smooth.

Spoon the beef mixture into a serving dish, gently spread the cauliflower mixture over the top, sprinkle with the remaining cheese and broil until the cauliflower mixture is golden, about 2 minutes.

LEGIT STEAK

MAKES: 5 servings

1 SERVING: 383 Calories, 31 g Fat, 2 g Carbs, 28 g Protein

||||||||||||||||||||||||||||||||||||||||||||||||

⅔ cup (160 ml) soy sauce

2 tbsp (15 g) brown sugar replacement (I recommend Swerve) or erythritol

½ cup (120 ml) olive oil

¼ cup (60 ml) lemon juice

5 cloves garlic, minced

3 tbsp (11 g) parsley

1 tsp chili powder

1 tsp black pepper

1¼ lbs (567 g) flank steak

The name speaks for itself. This steak is legit. Legitimately the only steak marinade you will ever need, featuring a balance of garlic and herbs with subtle sweet notes and a hint of tartness.

In a large zip-top bag, add the soy sauce, sugar replacement, olive oil, lemon juice, garlic, parsley, chili powder and black pepper. Shake well. Add the meat, pressing out as much air as possible, and shake well. Refrigerate for at least 5 hours, and up to 2 days.

Grill or bake the steak to your desired temperature. I prefer medium-rare, which is an internal temperature of 140°F (60°C). This is achieved by grilling over medium-high heat for about 3 minutes per side, or searing the steaks in a skillet for 2 minutes per side and finishing in a 400°F (204°C) oven for 3 to 5 minutes.

||||||||||||||||||||||||||||||||||||||||||||||||||||||||||||||||||||||||||

TIPS: If you are short on time, you can cook the steak once it has marinated for at least 20 minutes.

If you can't find flank steak, or you see a better-priced alternate cut, feel free to substitute!

LICK-YOUR-PLATE GOOD BURGER

MAKES: 4 burgers

1 BURGER: 428 Calories, 33 g Fat, 2 g Carbs, 31 g Protein

|||||||||||||||||||||||||||||||||||||||||||||||||

BURGERS

2 tsp (5 g) paprika

2 tsp (5 g) brown sugar replacement (I recommend Swerve) or erythritol

1 tsp dried minced onion

½ tsp salt

¼ tsp black pepper

½ tsp garlic powder

½ tsp basil

½ tsp red pepper flakes

1 lb (454 g) 85/15 ground beef

3 tbsp (45 ml) soy sauce

8 lettuce cups or leaves

½ tomato, sliced thinly

SAUCE

⅓ cup (80 ml) mayo

1½ tbsp (22 ml) sugar-free ketchup

1 tbsp (15 ml) white vinegar

1 kosher dill pickle spear

½ tsp erythritol

½ tsp onion powder

¼ tsp salt

Dash of freshly ground black pepper

Dash of cayenne pepper

"Welcome to Keto Burger, home of the Lick-Your-Plate Good Burger. Can I take your order?" I hope at least half of you get that reference. '90s nostalgia aside, this is a burger that could stand on its own without a bun or sauce. Seasoned to the max, it's beyond flavorful. Add on the show-stopping, lick-your-plate good sauce and it's game over.

To prepare the burgers, in a large bowl, combine the paprika, sugar replacement, minced onion, salt, black pepper, garlic powder, basil and red pepper flakes. Mix in the beef and soy sauce. Allow it to sit while you make the sauce.

To make the sauce, in a blender, combine the mayo, ketchup, vinegar, pickle, erythritol, onion powder, salt, black pepper and cayenne pepper. Blend on high for 30 seconds until smooth. Set aside.

Form four patties with the ground beef. Grill or pan fry to your preferred temperature. For medium-rare, cook over medium-high heat for 2 to 3 minutes per side. For medium, cook over medium-high heat for 4 to 5 minutes per side.

Assemble the burgers by placing a patty on a piece of lettuce, topping with the tomato and sauce and covering with another piece of lettuce.

AMERICAN GOULASH

MAKES: 5 servings

1 SERVING: 255 Calories, 8 g Fat, 5 g Carbs, 26 g Protein

|||||||||||||||||||||||||||||||||||||||||||||||||||

1¼ lbs (567 g) 90/10 ground beef

¼ cup (40 g) yellow onions, diced

3 cloves garlic, minced

3 cups (720 ml) water

1 (15-oz [425-g]) can tomato puree

1 (8-oz [225-g]) can diced tomatoes, with liquid

1½ tbsp (5 g) Italian seasoning

2 bay leaves

2 tbsp (30 ml) soy sauce

2 tsp (12 g) salt

½ tsp paprika

½ tsp black pepper

½ medium head of cabbage

Are you team American chop suey or team goulash? An age-old question for the masses. This dish is referred to using both names. Regardless of what you call it, it is universally accepted as delicious. This tasty dish has seasoned ground beef in an Italian red sauce with "noodles" simmered until the cabbage takes on the delicious flavors of the sauce while maintaining the texture of a noodle.

In a large Dutch oven or pan set over medium heat, cook the ground beef for 5 to 6 minutes, until browned and broken up. Drain the grease from the pan. Add the onions and garlic, stir and cook for 5 minutes until the onions are translucent. Stir in the water, tomato puree, diced tomatoes, Italian seasoning, bay leaves, soy sauce, salt, paprika and black pepper. Bring to a boil then reduce the heat and simmer, covered, for 15 to 20 minutes.

While the goulash is simmering, cut the cabbage into thin strips similar in size to an egg noodle. Add the cabbage to the pot and stir until well combined. Re-cover and simmer for an additional 20 to 25 minutes until the cabbage is cooked through. Remove the bay leaves before serving.

|||||||||||||||||||||||||||||||||||||||||||||||||||||||||||||||||||||||||||||||||||||||||

TIP: Instead of simmering for 20 to 25 minutes, put in a baking dish, top with mozzarella cheese and bake at 350°F (176°C) for 30 minutes.

GREEK MEATBALLS

MAKES: 6 servings

1 SERVING: 386 Calories, 33 g Fat, 3 g Carbs, 19 g Protein

|||||||||||||||||||||||||||||||||||||||||||||

MEATBALLS

½ lb (227 g) ground pork

¾ lb (340 g) ground beef

6 cloves garlic, minced

6 large mint leaves, finely chopped

1 tsp oregano

2 eggs

½ cup (80 g) red onion, minced

¼ cup (15 g) fresh parsley, finely chopped

1 tbsp (15 ml) extra-virgin olive oil

1 tsp salt

½ tsp black pepper

TZATZIKI SAUCE

½ cup (65 g) cucumber, deseeded and finely diced

⅓ cup (80 ml) canned coconut milk

⅓ cup (80 ml) mayo

1 tbsp (15 ml) lemon juice

1 tsp garlic, minced

2 tsp (2 g) fresh dill

This is one of my favorite meatball recipes—perfectly moist and slightly crispy—topped with a light and creamy homemade tzatziki sauce.

Preheat the oven to 400°F (204°C). Line a baking sheet with aluminum foil.

Prepare the meatballs by mixing the pork, beef, garlic, mint, oregano, eggs, red onion, parsley, olive oil, salt and black pepper by hand until just combined. Be careful not to overmix. Form ping-pong ball–sized meatballs—I like to weigh the meat then divide equally—and place the formed meatballs on the prepared baking sheet. Bake for 30 minutes.

Make the tzatziki sauce by combining the cucumber, coconut milk, mayo, lemon juice, garlic and dill. Stir well.

Drizzle the tzatziki sauce over the cooked meatballs.

BAKED STUFFED STEAK

MAKES: 4 servings

1 SERVING: 337 Calories, 22 g Fat, 3 g Carbs, 32 g Protein

||||||||||||||||||||||||||||||||||||||||||||||||||||||

1 lb (454 g) flank or hanger steak

1 egg yolk

1 cup (30 g) spinach

2 tbsp (18 g) Parmesan cheese, grated

1 tsp Italian seasoning

1 tsp garlic powder

½ tsp salt, plus more for sprinkling

½ tsp black pepper, plus more for sprinkling

¾ cup (84 g) mozzarella cheese, shredded

½ cup (100 g) Roma tomatoes, diced

2 tbsp (30 ml) olive oil

This isn't your typical steak dinner. Stuffed with a filling cheesier than a '90s rom-com, you will not be disappointed.

Preheat the oven to 425°F (218°C).

Butterfly the steak by lining a knife parallel to a cutting board and slicing through the center of the steak, stopping just short of cutting all the way through.

In a large bowl, lightly whisk the egg yolk with a fork, then add the spinach and Parmesan cheese and mix well. Add the Italian seasoning, garlic powder, salt, black pepper, mozzarella and tomatoes and thoroughly mix.

Evenly spread the mixture inside of the butterflied steak, being sure to leave a 1-inch (2.5-cm) border without any mixture. This will prevent any over-flowing when cooking. Roll the steak tightly and secure with damp tooth-picks or cooking twine, secured every 2 to 3 inches (5 to 8 cm).

Place the stuffed steak on a baking sheet or oven-safe dish and drizzle with the olive oil. Sprinkle salt and black pepper over the steak. Bake for 20 to 25 minutes, then turn the oven to broil and cook until the steak is seared and the cheese is melted, about 5 minutes (cook for an additional 3 to 4 minutes if you prefer well-done).

Allow the steak to rest for 15 minutes before slicing. This helps to lock in the juices.

TACO PIE

MAKES: 6 servings

1 SERVING: 409 Calories, 33 g Fat, 5 g Carbs, 24 g Protein

||||||||||||||||||||||||||||||||||||||||||||||||||

MEAT

1 lb (454 g) 80/20 ground beef

3 tbsp (45 g) taco seasoning (page 24)

2 tbsp (30 g) tomato paste

10 oz (280 g) cauliflower rice, steamed and drained

⅓ cup (80 ml) beef broth

½ cup (57 g) Cheddar cheese, shredded

CRUST

1 cup (104 g) almond flour

1 cup (113 g) Cheddar cheese

½ tsp salt

½ tsp garlic powder

¼ cup (60 ml) sour cream

2 large eggs

1 tbsp (15 g) butter

Once you ditch those store-bought taco seasoning packets, you won't turn back. The flavoring of the meat with the homemade seasoning is incredible, and the crust of this taco pie is the real star of the show! No need to have taco shells when you can have this masterpiece.

Preheat the oven to 400°F (204°C).

To prepare the meat, in a large pan over medium-high heat, cook the beef for 5 to 7 minutes, or until thoroughly cooked. Stir in the taco seasoning, tomato paste, cauliflower rice and broth, cover and simmer for 2 minutes, stirring occasionally.

To make the crust, in a medium bowl, mix the almond flour, Cheddar cheese, salt, garlic powder, sour cream, eggs and butter.

Pour the beef mixture into a 9-inch (23-cm) pie plate and sprinkle with the Cheddar cheese.

Spoon the crust mixture over the meat and smooth with a spatula. Bake until the cheese is bubbly, about 25 minutes.

|||||||||||||||||||||||||||||||||||||||||||||||||||||||||||||||||||||||||||||||||||

TIPS: Top with a dollop of sour cream and some homemade guac for extra fats!

This freezes well!

DECONSTRUCTED GARLIC STEAK KABOBS

MAKES: 5 servings

1 SERVING: 348 Calories, 24 g Fat, 5 g Carbs, 26 g Protein

||||||||||||||||||||||||||||||||||||||||||||||||

1¼ lbs (681 g) beef sirloin, cubed

8 oz (225 g) white mushrooms, cut into 1-inch (2.5-cm) pieces

1 green bell pepper, seeded, cored and cut into 1-inch (2.5-cm) pieces

½ red onion, cut into 1-inch (2.5-cm) pieces

1 tbsp (15 ml) olive oil

Salt and black pepper, to taste

3 tbsp (45 g) butter

2 tsp (6 g) garlic, minced

1 tbsp (5 g) fresh parsley, chopped small

Kabobs are a grilling staple. Anything on a stick is instantly tastier.

Turn the grill to medium-high heat.

Thread the beef, mushrooms, bell pepper and onion onto skewers. Brush with the olive oil and season generously with salt and black pepper. Grill the kabobs until seared, 4 to 5 minutes per side.

In a small pan over medium-low heat, melt the butter, add the garlic and cook for 1 minute. Remove the pan from the heat and stir in the parsley. Add salt and black pepper to taste.

Remove the meat and veggies from the skewers and toss in the garlic butter sauce.

*See image on page 110.

||||||||||||||||||||||||||||||||||||||||||||||||||||||||||||||||||||||||

TIP: You can use a broiler if you don't have access to a grill. Prepare the skewers as directed above, place on a baking sheet coated with olive oil and broil until seared, 4 to 5 minutes per side.

BIGGER FISH TO FRY

||||||||||||||||||||||||||||||||||||||||||||||||||||||||||||||||||||||||||||||||||||||||||||||||||||||||||||||||||||||||

In this chapter you will find fish and seafood recipes proven to make even the pickiest of eaters ask for seconds! From the ever-popular Tuscan Salmon (page 156) to the fresh and flavorful Roasted Greek Salmon (page 168), the flavor profiles will range from salty and sweet, to spicy, and back again in this amazing collection of crowd-pleasing seafood recipes that will make a splash at your dinner table!

TUSCAN SALMON

MAKES: 4 servings

1 SERVING: 443 Calories, 34 g Fat, 4 g Carbs, 31 g Protein

IIIIIIIIIIIIIIIIIIIIIIIIIIIIIIIIIIIIIIIIIIIIIIIIIII

1 tbsp (15 ml) extra-virgin olive oil

4 (6-oz [170-g]) salmon fillets

½ tsp salt

½ tsp ground black pepper

3 tbsp (45 g) butter

3 cloves garlic, minced

1 cup (200 g) Roma tomatoes, diced

½ cup (120 ml) half and half

¼ cup (25 g) Parmesan cheese, grated

2 cups (60 g) spinach, fresh or frozen

2 tbsp (5 g) fresh basil, chopped

2 tbsp (10 g) fresh parsley, chopped

½ tsp Italian seasoning

This creamy Italian delight will have you saying, "So long, spaghetti" and "Hello, salmon!" Flavorful, delicious and super easy to make—even the beginner cook can whip this one up!

Heat the olive oil in a large nonstick skillet over medium-high heat. Season the salmon with the salt and black pepper. Cook, skin side up, for 5 minutes, then flip and cook for 2 minutes. Transfer to a plate and set aside.

Reduce the heat to medium and melt the butter in the pan. Stir in the garlic and cook until fragrant, about 1 minute. Add the tomatoes and cook for 1 to 2 minutes. Add in the half and half, Parmesan cheese, spinach, basil, parsley and Italian seasoning and bring the mixture to a simmer. Cook for 2 minutes. Add the salmon back to the skillet and spoon with the sauce. Simmer until the salmon is fully cooked and flaky, about 3 minutes.

PECAN-CRUSTED MAPLE SALMON

MAKES: 4 servings

1 SERVING: 411 Calories, 23 g Fat, 1 g Carbs, 25 g Protein

||||||||||||||||||||||||||||||||||||||||||||

1 tsp olive oil

4 (4-oz [120-g]) salmon fillets

¾ tsp paprika

½ tsp salt

¼ tsp black pepper

½ cup (55 g) pecans, diced

2 tbsp (30 g) butter

2 cloves garlic, minced

1 tsp ground ginger

2 tbsp (30 ml) sugar-free maple syrup

1 tbsp (15 ml) lemon juice

1 tbsp (7 g) brown sugar replacement (I recommend Swerve) or erythritol

This perfectly crispy Pecan-Crusted Maple Salmon is sure to steal the show at your next dinner party. The sauce is sweet—with a subtle spiciness—and it creates a perfect glaze to seal in the moisture to make a flaky fish.

Drizzle the olive oil over the salmon fillets and sprinkle with the paprika, salt and black pepper. Evenly divide the pecans and gently press into the tops of the salmon.

Preheat the broiler.

In a nonstick, oven-safe saucepan, heat the butter, then add the garlic and ginger and cook for just under a minute. Add the maple syrup, lemon juice and sugar replacement and bring to a boil. Carefully add the salmon fillets to the pan and cook for 5 minutes. The salmon should be a nice, bright pink.

Put the pan with salmon into the oven and broil until the top is browned, about 3 to 5 minutes.

||||||||||||||||||||||||||||||||||||||||||||||||||||||||||||||||||||||||||||||||||||||

TIP: If you don't want to heat the house up, you could make foil packets and cook the salmon on the grill. Just be sure to first make the sauce on the stove, or sprinkle the ingredients evenly over the tops of the salmon, before grilling.

CREAMY ITALIAN SHRIMP

MAKES: 4 servings

1 SERVING: 451 Calories, 34 g Fat, 5 g Carbs, 32 g Protein

||||||||||||||||||||||||||||||||||||||||||||||||

2 tbsp (30 g) butter

6 cloves garlic, finely minced

1 lb (454 g) shrimp, peeled and deveined, with tails removed

¼ cup (40 g) yellow onion, diced

½ cup (100 g) Roma tomatoes, diced

1 cup (240 ml) heavy cream

¾ cup (180 ml) unsweetened almond milk

¼ tsp xanthan gum

Salt and black pepper, to taste

10 oz (280 g) baby spinach

⅔ cup (66 g) Parmesan cheese, freshly grated

2 tsp (4 g) Italian seasoning

1 tbsp (7 g) fresh parsley, chopped

When I am in the mood to impress, I always love to do a Keto spin on an Italian favorite, and this Creamy Italian Shrimp never fails to wow my dinner guests. Bursting with fresh flavor, this meal will have them drinking the sauce and wondering how they ever lived without this dish!

Place a large skillet over medium-high heat and melt the butter. Add the garlic and cook until fragrant, about 1 minute. Add the shrimp and cook for 2 minutes per side until cooked through and pink. Transfer to a bowl and set aside. Add the onion and tomatoes to the skillet and cook for 1 to 2 minutes. Reduce the heat to medium-low and add the cream and almond milk. Bring to a gentle simmer, stirring occasionally, then add the xanthan gum and continue to stir until thickened. Season with salt and black pepper.

Add the spinach leaves to the pan and allow them to wilt. Mix in the Parmesan cheese, allowing the sauce to simmer until the cheese melts, about 1 minute. Add the shrimp to the mixture and sprinkle with the Italian seasoning and parsley. Stir well.

CARIBBEAN SHRIMP

MAKES: 4 servings

1 SERVING: 330 Calories, 20 g Fat, 1 g Carbs, 28 g Protein

||||||||||||||||||||||||||||||||||||||||||||||||||||

⅓ cup (80 ml) olive oil

2 large cloves garlic, roughly chopped

1 jalapeño (seeded if you don't like spice)

1 tbsp (7 g) brown sugar replacement (I recommend Swerve) or erythritol

1 tsp paprika

1 tsp chili powder

1 tsp garlic powder

1 tsp onion powder

1 tsp cumin

1 tsp salt

½ tsp black pepper

3 tbsp (45 ml) lime juice

¼ cup (5 g) fresh cilantro, chopped

1 lb (454 g) raw jumbo shrimp, peeled and deveined

The first time I tasted Caribbean-style food was while scuba diving with domino whales. The captain of the boat made a simple shrimp ceviche with fruit juice and chilies. It was refreshing and full of flavor. I wanted to recreate this food experience, but with a bit more flair. Fresh cilantro and lime juice, mixed with garlic and jalapeño, gives this dish a crisp spiciness. The sweetener helps to balance the flavors.

Blend the olive oil, garlic, jalapeño, sugar replacement, paprika, chili powder, garlic powder, onion powder, cumin, salt, black pepper, lime juice and cilantro in a blender and blend well until there are no sizeable pieces. Pour the mixture into a zip-top bag, add the shrimp and shake well. Refrigerate for 2 to 3 hours.

Heat a grill or a pan to medium-high, remove from the marinade and cook the shrimp until slightly pink, about 3 minutes per side.

LEMON GARLIC BUTTER SCALLOPS

MAKES: 4 servings

1 SERVING: 270 Calories, 17 g Fat, 2 g Carbs, 27 g Protein

||||||||||||||||||||||||||||||||||||||||||||||||

2 tbsp (30 ml) olive oil

1 lb (454 g) scallops

Salt, to taste

Freshly ground black pepper, to taste

½ tsp paprika

¼ tsp red pepper flakes

3 tbsp (45 g) butter, divided

4 cloves garlic, minced

¼ cup (60 ml) chicken broth

2 tbsp (30 ml) lemon juice

2 tbsp (15 g) parsley, chopped

Scallops can seem intimidating to make at home—if you overcook them they become tough and flavorless, but this recipe is almost foolproof!

Heat the olive oil in a large pan or skillet over medium-high heat. When the oil is hot and sizzling, add the scallops in a single layer. Be sure not to crowd the pan. Immediately season with the salt, black pepper, paprika and red pepper flakes. Sear for 2 to 3 minutes, then flip and sear for 2 minutes until crisp, light brown and cooked through. Remove from the pan and set aside.

In the same pan, melt 2 tablespoons (30 g) of the butter, scraping up any browned bits left over from the scallops. Add the garlic and cook until fragrant, about 1 minute. Pour in the broth and bring to a simmer, cooking for 2 minutes. Add in the remaining tablespoon (15 g) of the butter and lemon juice. Remove the pan from the heat, add the scallops back in and warm through. Garnish with the parsley.

The Daily Catch 35p

& Chi

SWEET AND SPICY SALMON

MAKES: 4 servings

1 SERVING: 324 Calories, 24 g Fat, 1 g Carbs, 26 g Protein

||||||||||||||||||||||||||||||||||||||||||||

2 tsp (6 g) garlic, minced

2 tsp (4 g) ground ginger

2 tbsp (30 ml) extra-virgin olive oil

2 tbsp (30 ml) soy sauce

3 tbsp (45 g) chili paste
(I recommend Sambal Oelek)

¼ cup (40 g) green onions, chopped

3 tbsp (22 g) brown sugar
replacement (I recommend Swerve)
or erythritol

1 lb (454 g) salmon fillets, skin off

Salt and black pepper, to taste

1½ tsp (3 g) paprika

1 tbsp (15 g) butter

This is an incredibly easy salmon dish with an Asian flair. This flaky ginger salmon is seasoned to perfection and is delicious served over riced cauliflower or spinach salad.

In a pie plate, whisk together the garlic, ginger, olive oil, soy sauce, chili paste, onions and sugar replacement. Put half the marinade in an airtight container and store in the fridge.

Season the salmon with the salt, black pepper and paprika. Place the salmon in the pie plate, turning to evenly coat in the sauce, and cover with plastic wrap. Let it marinate in the fridge for at least 1 hour, and up to 36 hours.

Preheat the oven to 375°F (190°C).

In an oven-safe skillet set over medium heat, melt the butter. Sear the salmon for 2 to 3 minutes on both sides, brushing with the reserved marinade as it cooks. Transfer to the oven and bake until flaky, about 8 minutes.

ROASTED GREEK SALMON

MAKES: 4 servings

1 (6.4-OZ [180-G]) SERVING:
434 Calories, 37 g Fat, 4 g Carbs,
32 g Protein

||||||||||||||||||||||||||||||||||||||||||||

TOPPING

¼ cup (60 ml) olive oil

¼ cup (60 ml) lemon juice

2 cloves garlic, minced

1¼ tsp (2 g) oregano

½ tsp red pepper flakes

½ cup (75 g) feta cheese, crumbled

½ cup (100 g) cherry tomatoes, halved

¼ cup (45 g) Kalamata olives, pitted

¼ cup (33 g) cucumber, diced

¼ cup (40 g) red onion, diced

1 tsp dried dill

¼ tsp salt

¼ tsp black pepper

SALMON

1 lb (454 g) salmon fillets

2 tbsp (30 ml) olive oil

½ tsp salt

¼ tsp black pepper

Colorful and flavorful, this dish gives you all the Greek vibes! This salmon is one of my favorite dishes to prepare, and it always leaves me feeling like I just stepped onto the beaches of Santorini!

Preheat the oven to 375°F (190°C).

To prepare the topping, in a medium bowl, mix together the olive oil, lemon juice, garlic, oregano, red pepper flakes, feta cheese, tomatoes, olives, cucumber, onion, dill, salt and black pepper.

To make the salmon, in an oven-safe dish, place the salmon fillets skin side down and drizzle with the olive oil, salt and black pepper. Bake for 10 minutes then add the topping evenly over the fillets. Bake until pink and flaky, about 10 minutes.

||||||||||||||||||||||||||||||||||||||||||||||||||||||||||||||||||||||||

TIPS: I like to broil the salmon during the last minute, but this is optional!

The topping has so much flavor and is also great over chicken or shrimp.

DYNAMITE SHRIMP

MAKES: 4 servings

1 SERVING: 180 Calories, 9 g Fat, 0.5 g Carbs, 23 g Protein

|||||||||||||||||||||||||||||||||||||||||||||

1 lb (454 g) extra-large shrimp, peeled and deveined

3 tbsp (45 ml) mayo

2 tbsp (15 g) green onions, diced

1½ tbsp (22 g) chili paste

1 to 2 tbsp (7 to 15 g) erythritol

Salt and black pepper, to taste

This dish is DYNO-MITE. Sweet, spicy and a little bit creamy, this was inspired by one of my favorite P.F. Chang's recipes. It does not disappoint.

Place the shrimp on skewers and grill over medium-high heat until slightly pink, about 2 minutes per side. Mix the mayo, onions, chili paste, erythritol, salt and black pepper and brush over the shrimp when they have finished cooking.

|||||||||||||||||||||||||||||||||||||||||||||||||||||||||||||||||||||||||||||

TIP: If you aren't a shrimp fan, chicken is a great substitute. Cut the chicken into bite-sized pieces and put on skewers. The meat will need longer to cook, about 7 minutes per side.

PAN-SEARED TOMATO BASIL HADDOCK

MAKES: 4 servings

1 SERVING: 245 Calories, 13 g Fat, 5 g Carbs, 24 g Protein

||||||||||||||||||||||||||||||||||||||||||||||||||

1¼ lbs (567 g) haddock

½ tsp paprika

1¼ tsp (10 g) salt, divided

¾ tsp black pepper, divided

2 tbsp (30 ml) olive oil

2 tbsp (30 g) butter

½ tsp crushed red pepper flakes

3 cloves garlic, minced

1 cup (150 g) cherry tomatoes, halved

¼ cup (60 ml) white cooking wine or chicken broth

3 tbsp (5 g) basil

3 tbsp (45 ml) lemon juice

1 tsp lemon zest

3 cups (90 g) spinach, chopped small

This fresh fish dish is seared to perfection with a refreshing light white wine butter sauce. It pairs well with cauliflower rice, which helps to soak up the extra sauce.

Season the haddock with the paprika, salt and black pepper.

In a large, nonstick, oven-safe skillet, heat the olive oil over medium-high heat and sear the fish for 4 minutes on each side. Set aside.

Add the butter, red pepper flakes, garlic, tomatoes, wine, basil, lemon juice and zest to the skillet and cover. Cook for 3 minutes, or until the sauce begins to bubble, and add the fish to the pan and spoon the sauce over the fish. Cover, reduce the heat to low and simmer for 5 minutes. Add the spinach and cook for 5 minutes, allowing the spinach to wilt.

||||||||||||||||||||||||||||||||||||||||||||||||||||||||||||||||||||||||

TIP: If you can't find haddock, you can substitute any white fish, such as cod or bass.

SHRIMP FANTASTICO

MAKES: 4 servings

1 SERVING: 422 Calories, 31 g Fat, 9 g Carbs, 21 g Protein

||||||||||||||||||||||||||||||||||||||||||||||||

SHRIMP

1 lb (454 g) medium shrimp, peeled and deveined, with tails removed

1 tbsp (15 ml) olive oil

2 tbsp (30 g) chili paste

½ tsp salt

1 tbsp (15 g) butter

SAUCE

1 tbsp (15 ml) olive oil

¼ cup (40 g) onion, diced

1 tsp ground ginger

½ tsp garlic powder

2 tsp (4 g) curry powder

12 oz (355 ml) unsweetened coconut milk

½ cup (120 ml) chicken broth

½ tsp xanthan gum

3 tbsp (22 g) brown sugar replacement (I recommend Swerve) or erythritol

3 tbsp (45 g) sugar-free peanut butter

2 tbsp (30 ml) lime juice

2 tbsp (30 ml) soy sauce

1 tbsp (15 g) chili paste

½ tsp basil

¼ tsp black pepper

1 medium (196 g) zucchini, chopped into small pieces or spiraled

8 oz (225 g) broccoli florets, steamed

Fantastico is right! These shrimp are delicious—bursting with a curry flavor that will send your taste buds on a holiday.

To make the shrimp, in a medium bowl, combine the shrimp, olive oil, chili paste and salt. Add the butter to a large skillet set over medium-high heat, discard the shrimp marinade and cook the shrimp for 3 minutes, then flip and cook for another 2 to 3 minutes until cooked through. You may have to work in two batches. Remove the shrimp from the pan and place it on a plate while you prepare the sauce.

To prepare the sauce, using the same skillet, heat the olive oil over medium-high heat, add the onion and cook for 3 minutes. Add the ginger, garlic powder and curry powder, and sauté for 1 minute. Turn the heat to low and add the coconut milk, broth, xanthan gum, sugar replacement, peanut butter, lime juice, soy sauce, chili paste, basil and black pepper. Mix well, then stir in the zucchini and broccoli. Cover and simmer for 10 minutes. Return the shrimp to the pan and simmer for an additional 5 minutes.

Sweet Dreams are
MADE OF THESE

||||||||||||||||||||||||||||||||||||||||||||||||||||||||||||||||||||||||||||||||||||||||||||||||||||||

For me, making Keto my lifestyle meant I NEEDED to find a way to incorporate a daily sweet into my life to satisfy my sweet tooth and—more importantly—keep me on track! The Whoopie Pies (page 178), OMG Bars (page 186) and Cream Cheese Brownie for One (page 194) should give you hope that not only is Keto doable, it's downright delicious!

WHOOPIE PIES

MAKES: 12 servings

1 SERVING: 233 Calories, 21 g Fat, 3 g Carbs, 7 g Protein

|||||||||||||||||||||||||||||||||||||||||||||||

COOKIE

½ cup (120 g) butter, softened

1 cup (125 g) powdered erythritol

3 large eggs

2 cups (208 g) almond flour

½ cup (45 g) unsweetened cocoa powder

2 tbsp (15 g) coconut flour

2 tsp (9 g) baking powder

¼ tsp salt

2 tsp (10 ml) vanilla extract

⅓ cup (80 ml) unsweetened almond milk

FROSTING

8 oz (225 g) cream cheese, softened

½ cup (60 g) powdered erythritol

½ tsp vanilla extract

3 tbsp (45 g) butter

2 tbsp (30 ml) unsweetened almond milk

This is a staple New England dessert. For those who have never heard of a whoopie pie, imagine two perfect cupcakes sandwiching delicious frosting between. Basically, holding perfection in your hands!

Preheat the oven to 325°F (162°C). Line two baking sheets with parchment paper.

To make the cookies, in a large bowl, beat the butter and erythritol until smooth, then beat in the eggs, one at a time. In a separate bowl, combine the almond flour, cocoa powder, coconut flour, baking powder and salt. Add the flour mixture to the wet ingredients and stir well to combine. Add the vanilla and almond milk. Mix well.

Roll out 24 (1-inch [2.5-cm]) balls of dough. Drop them onto the baking sheets to flatten the bottom. Bake for 12 minutes. Be sure to not overbake. They will harden as they cool.

While the cookies are baking, prepare the frosting. In a blender, add the cream cheese, erythritol, vanilla, butter and almond milk. Blend on high until whipped. Place the frosting in the fridge.

Allow the cookies to cool for 30 minutes. To assemble the pies, evenly distribute the frosting onto 12 of the cookies and sandwich with the remaining cookies.

THAT DOUGH THOUGH
COOKIE DOUGH FAT BOMBS

MAKES: 17 fat bombs

1 FAT BOMB: 175 Calories, 2 g Carbs, 16 g Fat, 3 g Protein

||||||||||||||||||||||||||||||||||||||||||||||||||

1 (8-oz [225-g]) block full-fat cream cheese, softened

1 stick (120 g) butter, softened

½ cup (60 g) erythritol

½ cup (85 g) sugar-free or low-carb chocolate chips, or 85% cocoa chocolate bar, chopped

2½ tsp (12 ml) vanilla extract

½ cup (110 g) peanut butter (made from peanuts and salt only)

Go ahead and eat that cookie dough! These are delicious and full of great fats.

In a mixer, combine the cream cheese, butter, erythritol, chocolate chips, vanilla and peanut butter. Cover the mixture and refrigerate for 1 hour.

Scoop the mixture into balls using a spoon or cookie scoop and place on a cookie sheet. Freeze for 2 hours. Transfer to a zip-top bag and store in the freezer.

BAKERY-STYLE CHOCOLATE CHIP COOKIES

MAKES: 12 cookies

1 COOKIE: 154 Calories, 4 g Carbs, 14 g Fat, 3 g Protein

||||||||||||||||||||||||||||||||||||||||||||||||

5½ tbsp (82 g) butter

⅓ cup (40 g) brown sugar replacement (I recommend Swerve) or erythritol

⅓ cup (40 g) erythritol

1 large egg

1½ tsp (8 ml) sugar-free chocolate syrup (I recommend ChocZero), sugar-free pancake syrup or erythritol

1½ tsp (8 ml) vanilla extract

1¼ cups (130 g) almond flour

1 tbsp (7 g) ground flaxseed

1½ tsp (7 g) baking powder

4 tbsp (18 g) unsweetened shredded coconut

½ tsp salt

½ cup (85 g) sugar-free chocolate chips

Sometimes you just need that simple, delicious, dunk-in-an-ice-cold-glass-of-milk—almond milk, of course—cookie. And this bakery-style cookie delivers!

Preheat the oven to 325°F (162°C). Prepare two baking sheets with parchment paper. Alternatively, you can grease the baking sheets or use silicone baking sheets.

In a large mixing bowl, with an electric mixer, cream the butter, sugar replacement and erythritol. Add the egg, syrup and vanilla, and continue to mix. In a separate large mixing bowl, combine the almond flour, flaxseed, baking powder, coconut and salt, and stir until combined.

Add the dry ingredients to the wet ingredients and mix until combined. Fold in the chocolate chips. Drop the dough by rounded spoonfuls onto the prepared baking sheets, spacing 1½ inches (3.8 cm) apart. Bake for 12 to 15 minutes, or until the cookies are browned on the bottoms. Let cool for 5 minutes.

CHOCOLATE PEANUT BUTTER FAT BOMBS

MAKES: 15 fat bombs
1 FAT BOMB: 66 Calories, 6 g Fat,
1 g Carbs, 2 g Protein

IIIIIIIIIIIIIIIIIIIIIIIIIIIIIIIIIIIIIIIIIII

BALLS

¼ cup (26 g) almond flour

¼ cup (55 g) sugar-free peanut butter

2 oz (60 g) cream cheese

4 tbsp (30 g) powdered erythritol

CHOCOLATE DIP

2 tsp (10 ml) MCT oil or melted butter

4 pieces (30 g) 100% unsweetened baking chocolate

1½ tbsp (12 g) powdered erythritol, plus more as needed

Simple desserts are often the best desserts. These fat bombs are one of the OG Keto4Karboholics recipes. Similar to a buckeye, these perfectly portioned morsels have just the right amount of sweet to end your day! And with macros this good, you can always fit in at least one.

Line a tray with parchment paper.

To make the balls, using a hand or stand mixer, combine the almond flour, peanut butter, cream cheese and erythritol. Make tablespoon-sized (16-g) balls with the dough. If you have a kitchen scale, you can weigh and divide equally into 15 balls; otherwise, eyeball the best you can. Place on the prepared tray and freeze for at least 20 minutes until hardened.

Prepare the chocolate dip by melting the MCT oil and chocolate in a microwave-safe dish and microwaving in 30-second intervals until melted. Stir in the erythritol, adding more or less depending on your preference, and allow the chocolate to cool for a minute.

Drop the balls into the chocolate dip, making sure they are completely covered, and place on the tray. Freeze for at least 30 minutes. Transfer to a zip-top bag and store in the freezer.

IIIIIIIIIIIIIIIIIIIIIIIIIIIIIIIIIIIIIIIIIIIIIIIIIIIIIIIIIIIIIIIIIIIIIIIIIIIIII

TIPS: If you want to make it easier, you can mix the melted chocolate into the batter instead of dipping the balls into the chocolate.

Almond butter can be substituted for the peanut butter.

CANDY BAR FAT BOMBS

MAKES: 20 fat bombs
1 FAT BOMB: 91 Calories, 8 g Fat,
1 g Carbs, 2 g Protein

||||||||||||||||||||||||||||||||||||||||||||||||||

BALLS

½ cup (120 g) cream cheese

1 cup (104 g) almond flour

¼ cup (18 g) unsweetened
coconut flakes

½ tsp vanilla extract

¼ tsp almond extract

Dash of salt

TOPPING

¼ cup (25 g) almonds, crushed

¼ cup (18 g) unsweetened coconut
flakes

2 tbsp (15 g) powdered erythritol

CHOCOLATE COATING

½ cup (85 g) sugar-free chocolate
chips or 85% dark chocolate,
chopped

2 tsp (10 ml) MCT oil

These fat bombs will have you reminiscing about your favorite almond and coconut candy bar, but without any of that guilt!

Line a plate with parchment paper.

Prepare the balls by combining the cream cheese, almond flour, coconut flakes, vanilla, almond extract and salt in a small bowl. Mix well, cover the bowl and freeze for 5 minutes. Separate the dough into 20 equal pieces—a bit smaller than golf balls—and roll into balls. Freeze on the prepared plate for 30 minutes.

Prepare the topping by combining the almonds, coconut flakes and erythritol in a small pie plate. Set aside.

To make the chocolate coating, melt the chocolate chips and MCT oil in the microwave in 30-second intervals, stirring in between, until the chocolate has melted.

Once the balls are frozen, dip each ball into the chocolate coating and roll into the topping. Return to the parchment-lined plate and freeze for 30 minutes. Store in a zip-top bag in either the freezer or fridge.

||||||||||||||||||||||||||||||||||||||||||||||||||||||||||||||||||||||||||||||||||

TIP: To make these dairy-free, substitute almond butter for the cream cheese and use vegan chocolate.

OMG BARS

MAKES: 10 bars

1 BAR: 264 Calories, 24 g Fat, 4 g Carbs, 4 g Protein

||||||||||||||||||||||||||||||||||||||||||

CRUST

½ cup (52 g) almond flour

2 tbsp (13 g) coconut flour

¼ cup (30 g) powdered erythritol

2 tbsp (30 g) butter, melted

1 tbsp (15 ml) vanilla extract

1 egg

FILLING

¼ cup (60 g) butter

6 tbsp (45 g) erythritol

2 tbsp (15 g) brown sugar replacement (I recommend Swerve), erythritol or monk fruit

½ cup (120 ml) heavy cream

1 tbsp (15 ml) vanilla extract

½ tsp xanthan gum

½ tsp salt

¼ cup (55 g) sugar-free peanut butter

TOPPING

1 cup (150 g) sugar-free chocolate chips

2 tbsp (30 g) butter

These are aptly named. You'll see why. A crumbly cookie crust layered with smooth peanut butter and finished with decadent chocolate. It's a combination that is going to have you saying OMG.

Preheat the oven to 350°F (176°C).

Make the crust by combining the almond flour, coconut flour, erythritol, butter, vanilla and egg. Mix well and press the mixture into an 8 x 8–inch (20 x 20–cm) pie pan or another oven-safe dish similar in size. Bake for 10 to 15 minutes, until golden. Keep an eye on the crust around the 10-minute mark to be sure it isn't burning. Allow to cool completely.

To make the filling, in a large pot over medium-high heat, stir together the butter, erythritol, sugar replacement, cream, vanilla, xanthan gum and salt and bring to a boil. Reduce the heat to a simmer for 1 minute then add in the peanut butter. Remove from the stove and cool for 5 minutes. Pour onto the cooled crust.

To make the topping, in a medium, microwave-safe bowl, melt the chocolate chips and butter in 30-second intervals, stirring in between, until smooth and melted. Pour over the peanut butter filling, cover and freeze for 2 hours. Cut into bars and store in the fridge or freezer.

||||||||||||||||||||||||||||||||||||||||||||||||||||||||||||||||||||||||||||||||||||||

TIP: Chunky peanut butter gives these an almost Snickers-like taste!

STRAWBERRY SHORTCAKE FOR TWO

MAKES: 2 servings

1 SERVING: 261 Calories, 25 g Fat, 4 g Carbs, 6 g Protein

||||||||||||||||||||||||||||||||||||||||||||||

SHORTCAKE

1 tbsp (15 g) butter

1 tbsp (15 ml) unsweetened almond milk

1 tbsp (15 ml) sour cream

1 tsp vanilla extract

1 tbsp (7 g) powdered erythritol

1 egg

¼ tsp baking powder

1 tbsp (7 g) coconut flour

2 tbsp (13 g) almond flour

TOPPING

¼ cup (60 ml) heavy cream

1 tbsp (7 g) powdered erythritol

¼ cup (38 g) strawberries, sliced

This is such an easy recipe to whip up when you are in the mood for something sweet. This dessert combines a light and fluffy shortcake topped with fresh whipped cream and sweet berries in perfect-sized portions for you and a friend.

Grease two 6-ounce (180-ml) microwave-safe ramekins.

To make the shortcakes, in a medium, microwave-safe bowl, melt the butter. Add the almond milk, sour cream, vanilla, erythritol and egg, whisking to combine. Add the baking powder, coconut flour and almond flour, whisking to combine.

Pour the mixture evenly between the ramekins. Microwave for 60 seconds and check for doneness by inserting a toothpick to see if it comes out clean. If additional cooking is needed, microwave for 30 seconds and check again. Allow to cool.

Make the topping by whipping the heavy cream until soft peaks form. Mix in the erythritol. Spoon the whipped cream and strawberries over the cooled shortcakes.

DOUBLE CHOCOLATE CHIP COOKIES

MAKES: 36 cookies

1 COOKIE: 145 Calories, 13 g Fat, 2 g Carbs, 3 g Protein

||||||||||||||||||||||||||||||||||||||||||||||||||||

1 cup (240 g) butter, softened

2¼ cups (270 g) powdered erythritol or monk fruit

2 eggs

1 tbsp (15 ml) vanilla extract

2 cups (208 g) almond flour

¾ cup (66 g) unsweetened cocoa powder

1½ tsp (7 g) baking soda

1 tsp xanthan gum

1 tsp salt

2 cups (335 g) sugar-free chocolate chips

Almost brownie-like in taste, but crispy in texture, these Double Chocolate Chip Cookies are the perfect bakery-style cookie.

Preheat the oven to 350°F (176°C). Line two baking sheets with parchment paper.

Using a mixer, cream the butter and erythritol until smooth. Add the eggs, one at a time, and continue to mix. Add the vanilla.

In a separate, medium-sized bowl, sift the almond flour, cocoa powder, baking soda, xanthan gum and salt. Add the dry ingredients in batches to the wet mixture, mixing until well blended. Gently fold in the chocolate chips.

Scoop 1-tablespoon (16-g) portions of the dough onto the baking sheet and cook for 12 to 14 minutes. They may look like they aren't fully cooked, but they will harden as they cool. Allow to cool for 2 to 5 minutes before eating.

|||||||||||||||||||||||||||||||||||||||||||||||||||||||||||||||||||||||||||||

TIPS: The dough can be frozen if you don't want to make them all at once. The baked cookies also freeze well.

These are GREAT with white chocolate chips. ChocZero and Bake Believe make sugar-free ones.

CHURRO CAKE FOR ONE

MAKES: 1 cake

1 CAKE: 363 Calories, 29 g Fat, 4 g Carbs, 9 g Protein

||||||||||||||||||||||||||||||||||||||||

CAKE

1 tbsp (15 g) butter, melted

2 tbsp (15 g) brown sugar replacement (I recommend Swerve), erythritol or monk fruit

1 tbsp (7 g) coconut flour

½ tsp baking powder

1 egg

½ tsp vanilla extract

¼ tsp cinnamon

TOPPING

2 tbsp (16 g) sugar-free chocolate chips

1 tsp butter

1 tsp brown sugar replacement (I recommend Swerve), erythritol or monk fruit

¼ tsp cinnamon

This fluffy and deceivingly filling churro-inspired mug cake, topped with a chocolate ganache frosting, is perfect for battling those snack attacks. The fact you can whip it up in under 5 minutes is just an added bonus. Now rapido, off to the kitchen.

Grease one 4- to 6-ounce (120- to 180-ml) microwave-safe ramekin or coffee mug.

To make the cake, mix together the butter, sugar replacement, coconut flour, baking powder, egg, vanilla and cinnamon. Pour into the ramekin and microwave for 1 minute. Remove to a plate.

Prepare the topping by combining the chocolate chips and butter in the same ramekin and microwave for 30 seconds, until melted. Stir and drizzle over the cake. Sprinkle with the sugar replacement and cinnamon.

||||||||||||||||||||||||||||||||||||||||||||||||||||||||||||||||||||||||||||

TIP: To make this dairy-free, substitute coconut oil for the butter and use vegan chocolate chips.

CREAM CHEESE BROWNIE FOR ONE

MAKES: 1 brownie

1 BROWNIE: 285 Calories, 23 g Fat, 5 g Carbs, 11 g Protein

||||||||||||||||||||||||||||||||||||||||||||||

1 tbsp (7 g) coconut flour

4 tbsp (29 g) erythritol, divided

½ tsp baking powder

2 tbsp (11 g) cocoa powder

1 egg, separated, room temperature

½ tbsp (7 g) butter, softened

¼ cup (60 ml) unsweetened almond milk

1 oz (30 g) cream cheese

½ tsp vanilla extract

Rich and fudgy with a cream cheese swirl, this brownie is perfection. Add to the fact that this is portioned all for you, what more could a person want?

Preheat the oven to 350°F (176°C). Lightly grease an 8- to 10-ounce (240- to 300-ml) oven-safe ramekin or mug or two cupcake tins.

In a small mixing bowl, combine the coconut flour, 3 tablespoons (22 g) of the erythritol, baking powder and cocoa powder. Mix well. Add the egg white, butter and almond milk and mix until a thick batter is formed. Pour into the baking dish.

In a small bowl, mix the egg yolk, cream cheese, remaining erythritol and vanilla. Pour over the batter and make a swirl in the batter with a knife.

Bake for 30 to 35 minutes, or until a skewer comes out clean from the center.

||||||||||||||||||||||||||||||||||||||||||||||||||||||||||||||||||||||||||||||||||||||||||||||

TIPS: If you have the macros available, top with fresh whipped cream or low-carb ice cream!

To make this dairy-free, substitute cold, whipped coconut cream for the cream cheese, or almond milk cream cheese. Use refined coconut oil in place of the butter.

CANNOLI FAT BOMBS

MAKES: 16 fat bombs

1 FAT BOMB: 161 Calories, 16 g Fat, 2 g Carbs, 3 g Protein

|||||||||||||||||||||||||||||||||||||||||||||||||||||

BALLS

8 oz (225 g) full-fat cream cheese

1 cup (225 g) ricotta cheese

1 cup (125 g) powdered erythritol

2 tsp (10 ml) vanilla extract

CHOCOLATE CHUNKS

1 cup (240 g) unsalted butter, melted

1 cup (88 g) unsweetened cocoa powder

1 cup (125 g) powdered erythritol

2 tsp (10 ml) vanilla extract

When you are from New England, you hold a few things dear: the Red Sox, the Patriots and a cannoli from Mike's Pastry in Boston. The cannoli is a true Italian dessert—sweet custard inside a crispy shell. I knew I needed to make my own version, so these chocolaty, creamy fat bombs came along and I said arrivederci to the carbs.

Line two trays or plates with parchment paper.

Using a stand mixer or hand mixer, mix the cream cheese, ricotta cheese, erythritol and vanilla until creamy and well mixed. Scoop the dough out into sixteen equal servings, about 2 rounded tablespoonfuls (28 g) each, onto one of the prepared trays. Freeze for 20 minutes, then form into balls. Return to the freezer.

Prepare the chocolate chunks by combining the butter, cocoa powder, erythritol and vanilla in a blender and blending well. Spread the mixture onto the other prepared tray and smooth to ¼-inch (6-mm) thickness. Freeze for 20 minutes. Once the chocolate has hardened, chop into small bits.

Roll the cannoli balls into the chocolate chunks, making sure the chocolate is pressed well into the balls. Store in the fridge for up to 1 month.

|||||||||||||||||||||||||||||||||||||||||||||||||||||||||||||||||||||||||||||||||||||||||||||||

TIP: You can substitute sugar-free chocolate chips instead of making the homemade chocolate chunks.

SNICKERS CHIA SEED PUDDING

MAKES: 1 serving

1 SERVING: 352 Calories, 30 g Fat, 4 g Carbs, 9 g Protein

||||||||||||||||||||||||||||||||||||||||||||||||

2 tbsp (20 g) chia seeds

½ cup (120 ml) unsweetened almond milk

½ tsp vanilla extract

1 tbsp (15 g) sugar-free peanut butter

1 tbsp (15 ml) Caramel Sauce (page 27)

1 tbsp (7 g) sugar-free chocolate chips

Erythritol, to taste

When you need something sweet but don't want to be hungry again in 15 minutes, turn to this fiber-packed dessert. Simple enough to make, and subtly sweet, this pudding will take care of your chocolate bar craving.

Simply combine the chia seeds, almond milk, vanilla, peanut butter, caramel sauce, chocolate chips and erythritol in a small Tupperware® or Mason jar and mix well. Cover and place in the fridge overnight.

||||||||||||||||||||||||||||||||||||||||||||||||||||||||||||||||||||||||||||||||||||||||||||||||||||||||||

TIP: The pudding will keep well for 3 days in the fridge. Make a few!

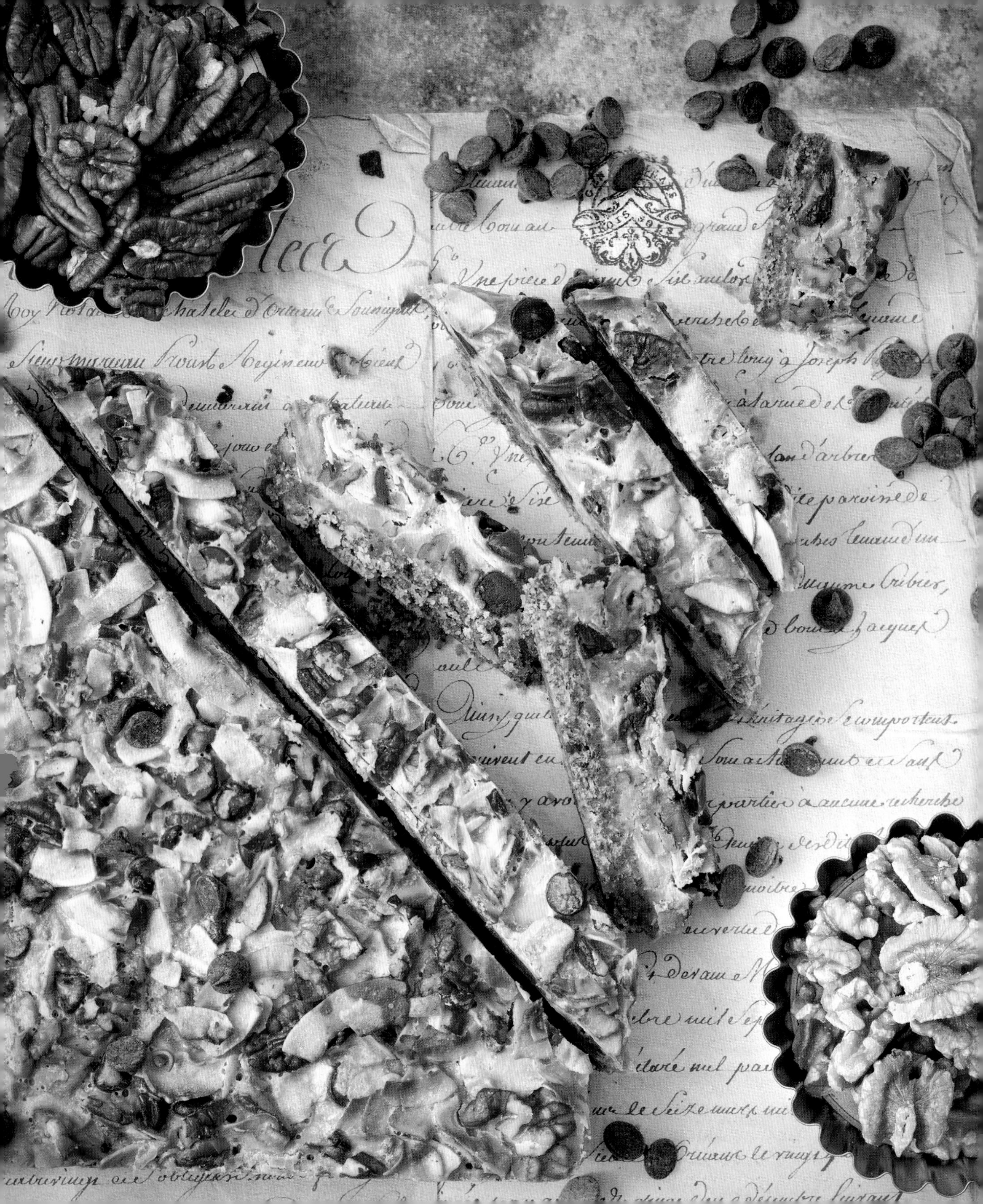

SERIOUSLY-EVEN-BETTER MAGIC BARS

MAKES: 20 bars

1 BAR: 354 Calories, 34 g Fat, 4 g Carbs, 5 g Protein

||||||||||||||||||||||||||||||||||||||||||

CRUST

½ cup (52 g) ground flaxseed

½ cup (52 g) almond flour

¼ cup (26 g) coconut flour

½ cup (120 g) walnuts, diced

½ cup (120 g) butter

1 tbsp (15 ml) vanilla extract

CONDENSED MILK

1 cup (240 ml) heavy cream

8 tbsp (120 g) butter

2 tbsp (30 ml) vanilla extract

1 cup (125 g) brown sugar replacement (I recommend Swerve) or erythritol

4 egg yolks

TOPPING

1½ cups (108 g) unsweetened coconut flakes

½ cup (75 g) sugar-free chocolate chips

1 cup (240 g) walnuts, chopped

1 cup (125 g) pecans, chopped

A family favorite recipe made healthy, these sweet, crunchy and chocolaty bars are the perfect mix for a dessert. Add in caramelized condensed milk and they are so magical.

Preheat the oven to 350°F (176°C). Line an 8 x 8–inch (20 x 20–cm) baking dish with parchment paper.

To make the crust, combine the flaxseed, almond flour, coconut flour, walnuts, butter and vanilla in a large bowl. Press the mixture into the bottom of the baking dish. Bake for 16 minutes or until golden brown.

Prepare the condensed milk by bringing the cream, butter, vanilla and sugar replacement to a gentle boil in a large sauce pan over medium heat and cook, stirring frequently, until it is a light golden brown and thick enough to coat the back of a spoon. Remove from the heat and allow to cool to room temperature before stirring in the egg yolks. Do not put it in the fridge to speed up the cooling process.

Top by sprinkling the coconut flakes, chocolate chips, walnuts and pecans onto the crust, drizzle the condensed milk over the top, and bake for 20 to 25 minutes, or until set and golden brown.

Allow to cool completely. Chill in the fridge before serving. This will help prevent the crust from crumbling. Store in the fridge for 5 days or in the freezer for a month.

Acknowledgments

Fifteen years ago, if you'd told me that one day I would be publishing my own cookbook, I would have never believed you. This was partially because at that time I was a horrible cook—I literally ruined boxed brownies. But determination, trial and error and becoming a wife and mother transformed me into who I am today. And while I can't thank every person who has made an impact in my life and this book, I want to try to acknowledge at least a few of you. This book would not have ever been a reality without the following people.

First, to my husband, Eric. As a health care provider, he was one of the first to introduce me to the Ketogenic diet. His work and research in treating a Type II DM patient with a Ketogenic diet inspired me to want to make a healthy change in our lives. His support for Keto4Karboholics was more than just financial—trust me when I say sometimes it takes many fails in the kitchen to make a winner, and ingredients aren't free. He pushed me to share my journey with others and open myself up by sharing my struggles, victories and delicious recipes. He has also been vital to this book's research, and he has become my lead taste tester. More than anything, he has been my best friend and kept me sane throughout my entire journey. I love you.

Thank you to my two children, Aryia and Cooper. They are honest to a fault, and my toughest critics. Thank you for letting your mom know when things were gross. I am sure the readers appreciate you screening the recipes for them. They have been amazing in sharing their mom, and even helping by typing on my laptop—doing "puter" work—in the middle of a deadline.

Thank you to Robyn, my amazing mother-in-law. I am so lucky to have a friend in you. The behind-the-scenes support that you give by coming over and helping to tackle the sheer craziness of the dirty dishes I make daily in my attempts to create delicious masterpieces. Helping me with the kids and letting me catch up on sleep when I work late, gossiping with me when I need a break and need adult conversation and just being there. I couldn't do this without you.

Grandma. You know I couldn't forget you. A strong, independent woman that has supported my dreams since I was a child. Always pushing me to do my best and telling me that I would be great. The never-ending support from you has got me to where I am today. You not only helped build my confidence, but you also helped me see that I can do whatever I put my mind to. While I am sorry this isn't the mystery novel you wanted from me, I know you will still read it and tell your friends about it.

Morgan, my baby sister. You keep me hip and tuned into pop culture, and without you I would be so behind the times and probably wouldn't have started an Instagram. But most importantly, you keep me organized. You are the woman standing beside me keeping me on task, simplifying my life and cheering me on. You win employee of the month . . . the century! You could never be replaced, and I am so happy to have you.

A very special thanks to Page Street Publishing. This process has been so smooth—and, dare I say, easy. For someone that has never written anything professionally besides research papers and proposals, I had no idea how to put a book out into the world. You reached out to me at the perfect time. I had wanted this book for some time, and you made this a reality for me. But even more, you allowed me to write this in a way I could stay true to myself and followers. Thank you so much.

Finally, to my followers and my challenge participants. The support I have received from you, the messages, transformation photos and everything you have shared and let me be a part of, have been my inspiration. We work together. We share and change each other's lives. You have become my friends. I look forward to our daily interactions—the jokes, the memes, the struggles. All of it. This has never been just a job for me. This is a calling, something I can't imagine not doing. Thank you for giving it to me. And thank you ALWAYS for being there. You are my biggest cheerleaders. And remember, "Keto works if you work it!"

About the Author

KASSEY CAMERON is a wife, the mother to two crazy children and the owner and face behind Keto4Karboholics, where she's helped over 70,000 men and women find support, education and guidance in making a lifestyle change to take back their health and lives. Kassey travels the world with her family looking for inspiration for her recipes, and she loves nothing more than enjoying time with her family in and out of the kitchen. When she isn't traveling or cooking, she can be found deep into research, attending medical conferences to learn about the newest research and impacts of the ketogenic diet in various fields and volunteering her time to help others. She lives in New Hampshire with her family, enjoying the short-lived summers and beautiful fall outside hiking, swimming and exploring.

Index